AMATORE MILLE

ELEVEN DAYS in AUGUST

A CHRONICLE OF SUMMERS

Trafford rev. 12/13/2021

North America & international
toll-free: 844-688-6899 (USA & Canada)
fax: 812 355 4082

To Dad -
YOU WERE RIGHT ALL ALONG.

ELEVEN DAYS

in

AUGUST

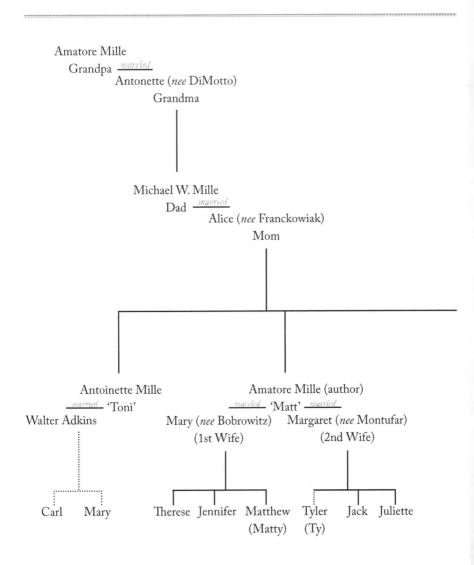

A State Fair Family

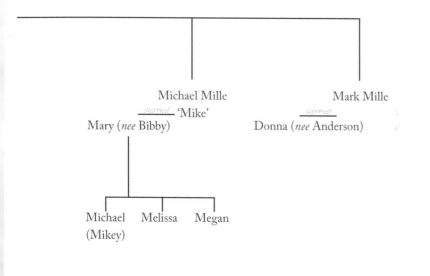

Michael Mille
married 'Mike'
Mary (*nee* Bibby)

Mark Mille
married
Donna (*nee* Anderson)

Michael   Melissa   Megan
(Mikey)

CONTENTS

INTRODUCTION

In August of every year members of the Mille family come together for eleven days to work in an annual business that has spanned four generations and, at last count, seventy-five years. They "vacation" from their mainstream jobs in Milwaukee, New York, Philadelphia and elsewhere to work eleven straight fifteen hour days under hot, smoky conditions with few breaks and little sleep - and they look forward to it each year.

This is the personal memoir of the author but, in a larger and more important sense, it is a family memoir as well. The Wisconsin State Fair, an annual event held in West Allis, Wisconsin, just outside of Milwaukee, has been a very popular regional event since 1892 - and Mille's Italian Sausage is the Fair's oldest and longest-running food concession. Begun in 1932 by my father, Michael, and his parents, Antonette and Amatore (my namesake), this family business is now run by my siblings and me. Our children, both grown and otherwise, represent the fourth generation of family actively involved in the business while a fifth generation is now beginning their apprenticeship as they learn the difference between sweet and sharp peppers, how to fill a cup with Coke (full but not so full that it spills when they carry it) and how to quickly but neatly wrap a sausage sandwich.

The Mille "family", it must be said, includes not just these direct descendants of the first Antonette and Amatore but many others as well. Over the years there have been many boys, girls, men, and women, who have - for eleven days of each year - become like family. One of them, in fact, having started as a young waitress at Mille's, has become an "official" family member through marriage. There's even been a Harley-riding dog[1] that joined our extended family for a couple of years. This memoir includes many remembrances of these important and interesting individuals.

Although this story is possible only because of the driving entrepreneurship of my grandmother (she, with her broken English, would not have know that fancy French/English word but her picture ought to be alongside it in Webster for she embodied the concept) - and much will be said about her - it is our father, Michael William Mille who was the soul of Mille's Italian Sausage from the earliest years, through the golden age of the Fair, and right up to his graceful departure soon after his last Fair in 2000. If this memoir warrants a dedication, it is to him that we all raise our sandwiches and remember every time one of us tells a new kid to not overfill a cup of Coke.

---

1   I mean no offense to the female companions of bikers – many of whom are our best customers with some actually being quite attractive. No, I am referring here to a true canine who rode a Harley Davidson, albeit as a passenger (after-all, she was only a dog). More on her in Chapter 3.

TRANSITION

THE MIDWEST FLIGHT LIFTS OFF THE RUNWAY IN PHILADELPHIA, bound for my home town of Milwaukee… and the attitude change is already beginning. It's an early Friday in August. My week has been hectic and it will take a while to decompress but I will make it - I always do. Packing my bag was a simple matter; lots of underwear, socks and shorts - no shirts necessary - there will be plenty of T-shirts awaiting my arrival. The big question was whether to laptop or not laptop. I decided to forgo the computer but bring a few of the files that I may need - just in case. Once I get in the swing of things I will probably forget all about the files and my job; after all, that's what vacations are for, right? The change I am about to go through is pretty extreme; earlier this week, at my regular job near Wall Street, I met with a business executive who runs a division of one of the largest financial institutions in the world - he has about 30,000 people under him. We discussed potential opportunities that could save his division millions of dollars - annually. Tomorrow morning, I will be getting crap from a Milwaukee teenager who wants sauerkraut on his $4.00 Italian sausage sandwich - and I will enjoy every second of it.

It hasn't always been this way. There were years - not many, but more than a couple - when I did not make it to the Fair and begrudged this week and a half as an imposition on my precious vacation allowance. Somewhere along the line, I finally managed to sort it out and gained perspective. I like to think I've got it all figured out now; maybe I do, maybe I don't, but I know that now I'm happy when I'm back at the Fair - and it has nothing to do with Ferris wheels or corn-on-the-cob.

On the plane with me is my stepson, Tyler, who's thirteen. This will be his first part-time job (if you can consider fifteen-hour workdays part-time work). Our flight will land soon and we'll arrive at the fairgrounds late in the evening but early enough to get into the swing of things and help close down for the night. So, I'm pretty-much ready to put on my Mille's Italian Sausage T-shirt and get back on that bike. I'll be in the groove in no time at all.

CHAPTER 1

HOW DAD HAD TO
GET HANDY FOR
ONCE IN HIS LIFE

FIRST WEEKEND: SATURDAY 8:55 A.M.

MY BROTHER MIKE'S CAR IS JAMMED WITH FAMILY, NEAR-FAMILY, and supplies. We're so packed in we must look like a group that thinks it's a carload day, a special one-price-pays-for-everyone day, which it isn't. We've already been up since 7:00 - very early considering we didn't get to bed till well after 1 a.m. (Fridays are late nights at the Fair). Entering the fairgrounds, we drive past the livestock barns, slowly threading our way around people and animals. As always, the early morning fairgoers with clean white sneakers, open sandals, and baby strollers are gingerly but good-naturedly navigating a minefield of horse and cattle manure. At the same time, farm kids with focused faces and appropriate footwear lead their Belgians and Swiss Browns to and from the livestock scrubbing areas - totally unmindful of what's underfoot and gradually adding to the complexity of the situation.

We now pass the postcard-perfect Anheuser Busch stables where smartly uniformed professional handlers are primping the Budweiser Clydesdales - and the Dalmatian too. Their presence, flaunted as it is, seems bold and arrogant - we are, after-all, in the Miller Lite country of Milwaukee. Anyway, I'm a Percheron man myself and I state my position to everyone in the car - as I do every year; I think they're tired of hearing it - in fact, I'm sure of it.

We've hauled in today's peppers, seventeen bushels (six sharp, eleven sweet) pan fried at six a.m. this morning by Mike's wife, Mary. It being Saturday we're expecting an early crowd and, weather permitting, a very busy day. Parking the car behind the stand[2], we tumble out and start opening-up. We each have our own routines which we go through without the need for discussion. Up go the window flaps, in come the day's fresh peppers and the Italian rolls and cannolis that are still warm from the Brady Street ovens of Sciortino's Bakery. The sausage truck is waiting for our arrival and the driver confers with Mike. They confirm the quantity and then the sausage, in ten-pound boxes, is hauled into the walk-in refrigerator.

Roy, our long-time sausage cook, is unshaven for yet another morning.

"Hey Matt, are you making coffee? Make it strong" he mutters.

---

2   From a time earlier then any of us can remember, the structure that houses Mille's Italian Sausage has always been referred to simply as "the stand". This term is probably a vestige of earlier times when we, like all of the vendors, used temporary, wood framed canvas roofed structures that were knocked down and stored away after each Fair. Since 1978 we actually have had two Mille's stands – the original permanent structure on Second Street, next to the corn roast, and a second, smaller stand in front of the Dairy Building. Always efficient in our communication, we simply refer to them as the "big stand" and the "small stand".

"Don't you worry Roy - I know how to make coffee the right way" I reply.

Roy, all tall and lanky, begins the important process of getting the charcoal grill ready for a busy day that will see several thousand sausages skewered and roasted alongside (never over) the unique Mille's grill. But first, the remaining ash and grease from yesterday's fire is shaken, poked, and scooped from the grill and hauled out in large ash cans used just for that purpose. Roy has now acquired the look of a true sausage cook through the addition of today's first layer of charcoal dust to his Mille's T-shirt, apron, and pretty much all of his exposed skin. By the end of the day numerous layers of dust will be laid down and, were he to die and require an autopsy, a good forensic pathologist could probably determine how many times he shook down the grill that day - maybe even over the last few days.

THE LATE 1930S

Michael William Mille is employed at a local manufacturing company but he is working hard on another business. Since 1932 he has been helping his mother and stepfather with their Italian Sausage sandwich business at the Wisconsin State Fair. Now, in the late 1930s, the sausage business is doing well but there is a growing concern that is keeping him awake even after long, hard days. The future of the business is threatened by the complaints of other vendors and the Fair administrators themselves. As Milwaukeeans discover Italian sausage and the popularity of the Mille's Italian sausage sandwich has grown, so has the problem of increasing clouds of smoke and fumes resulting from the roasting sausage juices dripping onto the live coals. The Fair has ended successfully for another year but he and his parents have been put on alert: the smoke problem will not be tolerated in the future. Since his parents are Italian immigrants who struggle with the English language, he is saddled with the responsibility of dealing with the problem or losing their promising business.

With this hanging over his head, he is faced with a true "necessity is the mother of invention" scenario. Unfortunately, he was never the handy type. He understandably struggles with this dilemma for some time as the start of next year's Fair rapidly approaches.

I like to think that he had a eureka moment, a sudden, thinking-out-of-the-box sort of breakthrough but, however it came to him, his radical idea promised to solve the smoke problem. Rather than cooking the sausages over a fire, he would turn the fire on its side and cook the sausages alongside it. That way, the sausage juices would still drip but not onto the live coals. Voila - no more smoky flare-ups

Now the challenge of design begins. With the start of summer, the Fair is drawing near. After numerous false starts and discarded design sketches, the final sketch is completed...here is a grill unlike any seen before. In thinking out-of-the-box, Michael has actually turned the box on its side. Picture, if you will, a wide, high, steel basket formed by wrapping and welding long steel straps around a steel frame which would hold the charcoal on a vertical rather than horizontal plane - a sort of wall of charcoal and fire about four feet wide and four feet tall. To this is welded an array of short, notched racks at both sides, front and back, and at various heights. To hold the sausage, simple spear-like instruments, more accurately referred to as "spits", are designed so that the sausages can be skewered vertically and packed tightly together along the length of the spit. The inventor is pleased with the design and is now ready to have the grill built by a local blacksmith. Soon, the construction is completed and now it is just a matter of waiting for the real test.

August arrives and advances and finally, in its third week, the eight day long[3] Wisconsin State Fair opens for another year and the baptism of fire, literally, is at hand. After a little tinkering and some fine adjustments–"fine" meaning the use of a small hammer rather than a big one – and with a full load of charcoal in the grill, Michael can now suspend the spits on the racks; there are about two dozen sausages on each spit – the busier it is, the more spits are hung ...and it works beyond all hope.

Not only is the smoke problem completely eliminated but, additionally, in a true incident of serendipity, an unintended benefit results: Fairgoers are now visually attracted by the sight of juicy sausages roasting at eye level, with each flip of the spits revealing their progress – from uncooked all the way to a "I want that-one-right-there; can you take that one off the spit for me?" state of completeness.

This unintentional "flash", as Michael liked to call it in later years, will become one of the trademarks of Mille's Italian Sausage, where the show of cooking is almost as important as the final product itself– in a perfect marriage of form and substance.

1941

On a warm July day, the inventor of the Mille's grill and savior of the upstart Italian sausage sandwich business marries his sweetheart of several years, Alice Franckowiak, the daughter of Polish immigrants.

---

3   The Fair has not always been eleven days long - its varied in duration over the years. In my own memory, the Fair ran for nine days, pre-1959. Nor has it run for an actual week, seven days, for all but a very few years. I don't know if the term "Fair week" is a vestige from those few years; that seems unlikely. I suspect the reason we , and many other Wisconsinites, refer to these eleven days as "Fair week", borrows from the "baker's dozen" sort of precedence - a little extra bonus of Fair days, if you will - but, regardless, even now we'll still ask each other, "when are you coming in for Fair week?"

His circle of friends envy his good luck in winning the affection of this most-attractive, black haired beauty but it's really no surprise for he, himself, is both charming and handsome - a deadly combination. Many years later, when looking at photos of him during this period, others will note his strong resemblance to a young Al Pacino, the future actor.

Michael and Alice will soon start a family of one daughter and three sons. I, Amatore, am the eldest of those three sons and my brothers are Michael (Mike) and Mark. Our sister, Antoinette (Toni), is the first-born.

SATURDAY 9:05 A.M.

Finding a measuring spoon and, after doing some quick math on a paper napkin, I start the ritual of making perfect coffee - exactly one and a half level tablespoons of properly ground Arabica coffee per six ounces of water; there's no measuring cup around, so I use a fourteen ounce Coke cup and adjust accordingly.

"What are you doin'?" a curious Roy asks as he dumps a bag of charcoal into the grill.

"Don't you worry, Roy, just take care of your fire; coffee's gonna be ready in a few minutes".

"I like it strong" he reminds me again.

"You are a royal pain in the ass" I tell him with an emphasis on the royal.

Smiling, he strides back to the grill in an odd and ungainly, forward-leaning but quick manner unique to himself (although Ichabod Crane comes to mind), and ignites the coals.

"When's Mikey coming in?" I ask my brother.

"Later this morning; he's driving down from Appleton" he tells me while cracking open rolls of quarters for the till. Mikey is Mike Jr., his son and grandson of our dad, Mike. Mikey is also father of little Michael, great grandson of dad and one of the youngest of the Mille clan - as well as of the four generations of Mikes. I'm the only one who refers to my thirty-year old nephew by the diminutive but I need some way of distinguishing among them all; too many Mikes in this place!

Mikey works as a pharmaceuticals sales rep and, like most of us, finds it difficult to work the Fair along with his day job. Having paid his dues as a State Fair sausage cook for many years, he now works just the weekends. It's not a lot but it keeps his grilling skills sharp and gives me and my sister Antoinette - who we call Toni most of the time - a chance to see him before she and I head back to our own day jobs on the east coast (from which we're officially on vacation). It also gives me a chance to tease him about whatever comes to mind. He gets to dish out his share of ribbing as well and likes to recount the time he subdued his uncle - humiliated, he says - in a wrestling match (the young man has a very overactive imagination; I advise people to humor him if he talks about it). It's all part of the appeal of Fair week.

"You working here today?" Roy asks.

"No, working at the small stand with Toni and Walter" I reply as I load a hand-truck with five plastic tubs of fried peppers and prepare to help them open up the other stand. Walter is my sister's husband; he and Toni came in early this year, as they do most years, to help get the small stand ready for the Fair opener. He'll go back to New Jersey after this first weekend. "Don't go pouring any coffee until its all brewed - and save some for me - I'll be back to get a cup after we get set up." Roy gives me an amused smile and shakes his head in acknowledgement. I hear him say something about the

Mom and Dad
– 1936

Dad "flashing"
a spit in 1983

Dad, Mom,
Mike, Grandma,
Amatore (author)
in "big stand"
– 1970s

Phillies and the Brewers as I walk away. I'll catch up on that later. Mark, the youngest of the Mille brothers, is helping stack the large boxes of Italian rolls in the backroom. I ask him if he brought along photos of the painting that he did for the Milwaukee Public Television Channel 10 annual auction; he was the featured Milwaukee artist this year and created a painting of the new Milwaukee Art Museum which he contributed to their fundraiser. He was interviewed, live, by the MPTV host during the auction and I hope to see a video of that as well.

"Yeah, I'll bring them over later, and I also want to ask you about fishing the small trout creeks in the southwestern part of the state". This comment floods my mind with memories of searching out the tiny, alder-shaded feeder creeks of Wisconsin where colorful native brookies can still be found.

"Great, I'll probably be seeing Ken early in the week; he's fished those streams" I say. "I'll let him know you want to talk to him." He's my old Wisconsin trout fishing buddy, the best kind. I knew he was the sort of person I could spend Saturday mornings with when he first took me, in the pre-dawn dark, to a certain central Wisconsin trout stream and showed me how to catch big-shouldered brown trout on an upstream cast. Even before full light, with a drake wood duck swooping through the woods to my left, there was a fifteen-inch brownie somersaulting at the end of my line. Of such things are memories and friendships made - at least of the trout fishing variety. Although its never arranged or discussed, I know that he and his wife will stop by to see me as they do every year, probably on Monday or Tuesday. We will recall stories of trout fishing and duck hunting with the fish getting bigger and the mythical northern flights of mallards and widgeon more plentiful with each year's telling.

Toni and I take the short stroll to the small stand, a trip we will repeat several times today and a great many times over the rest of the Fair. Early morning bustle prevails as delivery trucks, arriving employees, and fairgrounds clean-up crews scurry around like a colony of ants, each driven by the task at hand. An aura of anticipation is all-about and cheerfulness is thick. A quick "how ya doin'?" is exchanged with familiar faces we see every year, some for many years running. Juices from the fried peppers drip from the plastic tubs stacked on the tilted handcart I'm pushing and add to the permanent stain of pepper juices, a trail that connects Mille's Italian Sausage on Second Street with Mille's by the Dairy Building.

I like to think that archaeologists of the next century will puzzle over this strange stain on the pavement, not knowing it was created over the course of many years of Mille's pepper hauling. Although I've never suggested it, a person who needs directions from one Mille's stand to the other could actually follow the pepper juice line and get there in a very direct manner with no fear of getting lost. It's sort of like the way they use aerial photographs to locate ancient Native American sites on the mesa tops of the American southwest by spotting the faint trail remnants between them.

Toni, Walter, and I open the small stand and everything is done quickly and efficiently. She is a master of organization and is in complete charge of the kitchen and staff, make no mistake about it. I'm certain that if the FEMA organization was run by her there would be far fewer operational glitches. I, myself, oversee the sausage cooking, including training new cooks and relieving them during their breaks. The cash register is also my responsibility, most days. Toni knows that after I complete my morning tasks I will go back for my coffee and grab a very quick breakfast somewhere, then return in a total of about twenty minutes so that she and Walt can do the same. Early morning is a special time of day at the Fair. The fairgrounds, always litter-free, are now still wet from their early-morning shower, compliments of the sprinkler truck, and are invitingly wide-open with only the earliest arrivals walking about. None of the day's crises is yet at hand. There will be plenty of them all week long but this is a time to just take care of familiar, automatic routines; it's work, make no mistake about it, but it's a no-brainer and provides the opportunity to chat with family, most of whom I haven't seen for a year. And so I head back to the big stand, soaking up the familiar atmosphere of a sunny Saturday State Fair morning with its sights, sounds, and smells all triggering deep, meaningful connections. The aroma of roasting whole pigs, rotating slowly over beds of live coals, mingles with that of corn on the cob, also roasting but, in their case, over the huge gas-fired grills of the New Berlin Lion's Club. A slight wind-shift brings the sound and smell of popping corn from one of the little red wagons that is getting its morning supply ready. At the livestock area, people are lining up to have an opportunity to milk a Wisconsin dairy cow, the old-fashioned way, and even the strong smells here are, to me, pleasant and, somehow, comforting.

Now, back at the big stand, I talk to Mark again about his trout fishing plans and step to the kitchen to get my coffee. Its been only twenty minutes since I set it up - but there's only a few ounces left in the pot. Turning to my left, I see, standing at the grill, Roy who looks well-coffee'd as he sips from a ridiculous, Big-Gulp sized mug. I'm already annoyed but I pour the remaining coffee anyway and give Roy a dirty look as I take a sip. It tastes very weak, suspiciously weak.

"Roy - what did you do to the coffee?"

"Huh, what?" He strides over, angularly, with a puzzled, concerned look on his stubbly face.

"The pot was getting low so I just added a little more water."

Now, I really like Roy and we do a lot of kidding back and forth, but now I'm truly pissed and I tell him so in words that could not be said to most employees without getting in trouble. I make my point and he promises to never mess with the coffee again. I make a fresh pot and, just for emphasis, describe the critical ratio of ingredients to him as I do so. I'll get over it by noon and he and I will tease each other about this for the rest of the Fair.

It's not even 9:30 and the first of today's customers, an elderly gentleman wearing a Brewers' cap, has already stepped to the counter and asked when the sausages are going to be ready. "This is my first stop, every year" is his familiar greeting, his way of saying it's good to be back at the Fair again. We'll hear that same welcome from others early this morning and every morning this week and we never tire of it.

"Come back in about fifteen minutes" my brother Mike says knowing that Roy is about to get a fresh spit started now that his fire is heated up.

After it's all said and done, it really is all about the sandwich at Mille's. From the earliest years, grandma and dad always stayed focused on selling the best possible Italian sausage sandwich. They had many opportunities to make more money by adding other high-margin products or by cutting corners on quality here or there but they never went down those paths. The most important ingredient is, of course, the sausage itself. Grandma and dad experimented with their recipe until they got it just right. Dad's education and grandma's many years of exposure to great Italian sausage undoubtedly were important. On the other hand, they never were in the sausage production business and always contracted with trusted partners who made the Italian sausage based on the secret Mille recipe. In the mid 1950's, as our popularity rose, we partnered with a new, growing Milwaukee-based sausage company that shared our philosophy on quality. That company, Klement's Sausage of Milwaukee, could also handle our growing production needs. Dad made the decision and they began to produce the sausage to our proprietary, secret recipe. They have been our valued partner now for about fifty years. Klement's has grown very significantly over those years and, although our business represents a very small portion of their overall revenues, they have never forgotten nor stopped appreciating the commitment that dad made to them so many years ago when they were still a struggling new company. It has been a valuable partnership.

Although the sausage is the main and most important part of an Italian sausage sandwich, you wouldn't have a sandwich without the bread and its quality can make or break a sandwich. In the old days we used French bread for the sandwiches. We would get very long loaves from Gardetto's Bakery which was a very small family business at the time…

1953

Flour is everywhere; the counters and floor look like a skylight was left open on a night that saw snow. We're inside Gardetto's Bakery on Howell Avenue picking up French bread and the smell is wonderful. Dad tells Toni, Mike and me to help carry the big brown bags of French loaves out to the car. He's driving mom's new, yellow 1953 Buick today and we manage to somehow stuff all the bread into the car.

Each bag has a dozen or more loaves of soft but crusty bread so fresh the paper bags are warm...almost hot... to the touch. The long, slim loaves are protruding a foot or more beyond the top of the bags. Toni is in the back seat with the bread while I'm sitting in the middle of the front seat with dad and Mike... who somehow got the window seat again. The smell and warmth of all that fresh bread in the car, so close to us, is overpowering as we begin to drive back to the fairgrounds. Dad, always a big bread man himself, has no objection to each of us tearing off a chunk to munch on while he drives. We've been enjoying the bread for a few minutes when dad stops at a red light. Idling there for few seconds, I notice that my little brother, who's five, has that look on his face - the one that he gets when he's stuffed and can't eat anymore. It's the same expression he had that night at Michaelangelo's, dad's new Italian restaurant, when, after drinking glass after glass of water, with a quick refill being provided each time by an overeager busboy, he finally said, "How much more water do I have to drink?" Only this time it's bread, not water that's filled him up. Before I know what he's doing, he flips the remaining hunk of French bread that he's been eating out through the open car window. He does it without even looking and I watch as the sizable chunk of crusty bread with its freshly-chewed-on texture tumbles end-over-end through the air, slow motion like...and into the open window of a car on our right, also stopped at the light. As the middle aged man in the driver's seat looks down at his lap to see what just landed there his eyes expand to the size of small pizzas and, even before he has a chance to look up, dad has stepped on the gas and shot through the intersection. The man in the car is never seen again. For years to come I will wonder what that guy thought at the time. Maybe he reported it as one of those bizarre phenomena like the raining of fish or toads. Fact IS stranger than fiction.

SATURDAY 9:45 A.M.

We have not used French bread for many years and we have had a long and successful relationship with Sciortino's Bakery on Brady Street. They have come up with a light, seeded Italian roll that is absolutely perfect for our Italian sausage. It complements the sausage without overpowering it and the size is just right. The French bread, in comparison, was much heavier and, while tasty in its own right, did not complement our sausage like Sciortino's rolls do. As if that weren't enough, they are also able to provide us with sliced rolls which saves us a lot of time and anguish. Before, using the long loaves of French bread required the cutting and slicing of all the bread on a daily basis, which was very labor intensive, and dangerous. I have grown daughters who still carry scars from those days. Most of the older Mille women, for that matter, have a few wounds from the old days.[4]

The final ingredient on a Mille's sausage sandwich is, of course, the peppers. We serve two types of peppers: a sweet, mild green bell pepper and, for those of a more adventurous bent, a moderately hot ("sharp") yellow pepper. The sharp pepper is often referred to as a hot banana pepper but its technically correct name is the Hungarian wax pepper. Sweet or sharp, that's the choice we have offered for seventy-five years and it's the first thing a new kid learns when they start to work for us at the Fair. The question, "sweet or sharp?" will be asked, usually exactly that way (but sometimes it's "hot or mild?" just to break up the monotony), thousands of times over the eleven days of each Fair. For the cognoscenti of Mille's

---

4   Lest the reader jump to a conclusion of gender discrimination, it must be pointed out, first, that this was a long time ago, and, secondly, the Mille men, most of them, have their own share of scar tissue, but mostly of the burn variety.

Italian Sausage, the "combination" is the ultimate. The blend of the sweet pepper with the hot-but-not crazy-hot bite of the sharp peppers with their respective juices mingling and complementing the flavor of the Mille's sausage and the perfectly-light Italian roll holding the whole thing together … ahhh Marone!

Now, that's the right way, but I must admit to a certain degree of family shame. After many years of telling fairgoers "No, we don't have ketchup or mustard" we finally gave-in years ago and began to offer little packets to those who felt they couldn't enjoy a sandwich, any sandwich, without one or the other or both. At times, I feel we've been enablers of a travesty… no…an abomination, for an Italian sausage sandwich should never be desecrated by such condiments. But even my trout fishing buddy Ken, an educated man who grew up in New Jersey, a state lousy with Italians and their sausage, and who ought to know better for God's-sake, has to put ketchup on his Mille's Italian sausage sandwich. I've given up on him and we've given up in general, but I fear that my family and I will someday have to answer for our enabling…for our weakness in the face of pressure. So, with this in mind, we implore our customers to enjoy our sandwich the right way, the Italian way… but if you must…!

CHAPTER 2

GRANDPA AND
THE COWBOY

SATURDAY 10:15 A.M.

"TWO SWEET, ONE SHARP" THE YOUNG GIRL SAYS, STILL TENTATIVELY, to the other teenager who's wrapping in the kitchen. We're starting to serve sandwiches and have settled into our routine for a long day. A few sets of young twins, each pair in identical cute outfits, walk by with their parents; no need to check the Fair program to understand what's being judged today. Glancing over my shoulder, I notice that the teen-aged boys working at the french fry joint next to us have begun to check-out the fifteen and sixteen-year old girls working in our stand; I can see trouble coming. I notice, too, that my precociously social and good-looking stepson Tyler, a six-footer who looks much older than his thirteen years, is already getting chatty with the kitchen girls. Trouble all around me, but for a teenager at the State Fair, life is good. Trouble or not, I'm pleased to see how well Ty is taking to working here; for a kid who can't seem to even pick-up after himself back home, he's all over things here on his first day at the Fair. His blond hair and fair complexion raises a question of ethnicity to which I simply tell people his family's from Northern Italy, which he quickly, and accurately, denies.

Cream puffs and their makers are everywhere. We have the side-benefit of being situated, here at the small stand, right beside the "stage door" of the State Fair Dairy Building where the fantastic whipped cream-filled, mile-high puffs are made by the gazillions. A constant stream of men, women, boys and girls are near our side counter, coming and going from their breaks, white-outfitted head to toe. The head of the bakers union manages the entire operation and, seeing each other for the first time this year, we chat for a few minutes - mostly just getting re-acquainted and talking about this year's Fair, what we might expect weather-wise, that sort of thing...mainly small-talk but there's a comfortable familiarity in it.

"Hey Tom" I call out and my smile widens as another old friend in white strolls to our counter. Tom is who I guess would be called the head baker; in any case, he's the manager's right arm guy and we've known him forever. Tom looks tired (hey, he's a baker!) but there's also a warmth in those weary eyes that is genuine and comes from the soul. He's just a really good guy and a pleasure to see every year. Last year - I think it was - he arranged for the delivery of four dozen cream puffs to our mom at her retirement home complex, thereby instantly elevating her social status. A relatively unknown newbie, she suddenly was approached by all sorts of potential new friends and eventually had to hole-up in her apartment till her newfound popularity waned. Such is the fame of Wisconsin State Fair creampuffs and the heart of Tom the baker. After a brief chat, he goes back into the Dairy Building and I turn back to my cash register to check my supply of singles. I know I'll see him a couple of times each day, coming and going, and it all feels right.

"Amatore!" Even before turning in my chair at the register, I know who the deep, male voice belongs to. Sure enough, there's my old Pius XI high school friend and track team buddy, Robb stepping up to the counter with a big smile on his face.

"Robb ....Good to see ya man!" I say as we shake hands and check out how well the other is aging - and I can't help but wonder if I'm doing anywhere as well as him in that department. Robb Edwards is a very popular radio personality here in the Milwaukee area. He's also the public address announcer for the Milwaukee Brewers, "the voice of the Brewers", as it were - a job he loves (who wouldn't?). He stops by to see me here at the Fair every year. It's easy for him to see me since he's usually doing a stint from the fairgrounds for WOKY - but it would be even easier for him to not bother, and I really appreciate his taking a few minutes to stay in touch.

Rob and I rehash our track team experiences and the practices we endured right here on the grounds of The Wisconsin State Fair. We would get started during the pre-season with "voluntary" distance conditioning that had us running through these very fairgrounds in the winter months, in baggy, gray sweat suits (this was years before today's stylish work-out suits), terry cloth towels wrapped around our necks for warmth. There was nothing lonelier or less motivating then Western Avenue, behind the sheep and goat barns, on the second mile of a cold December morning. We trained in these fairgrounds during spring, too. At one time, we practiced on the north end of the State Fair, about where the indoor Olympic speed skating track now sits. Later, we trained inside the "Milwaukee Mile", the oval mile track that is located here at the Fair, overlooked by the Grandstand. I still carry a nasty memento on my right shin from one of those practices. During wind sprints along the inner sports car track of the paved oval mile, I scrapped my leg against a torn and rusted metal retainer rail, the obvious vestige of some sports car crash (perhaps even involving local racing legend Augie Pabst in his Scarab?) that now claimed its second victim. Bloodied out of proportion to the actual damage done, I was rushed off to the County Hospital emergency room for attention. The Milwaukee Mile holds other memories for me as well…

1959

It was all Richie's idea and it seemed like a good one, at the time. His ideas always seemed good, or at least exciting. Definitely exciting. Together, we'd gone to a sports car race at the State Fair track and seen Augie Pabst negotiate that hairpin turn on the inner track. Now, we had the go-kart, the one dad bought for my brothers and me, going around our driveway so fast that the State Fair hairpin would be easy enough, even for us kids. Richie and I were best buddies, had been for a couple of years. His family moved into our parish two years earlier and we met as seventh graders on the playground at St. Anthony of Padua, right across from Pius XI where we both later went to high school.

"Wanna race to the building?" the cocky new kid in my seventh grade class had asked me during recess that first school day in 1957. He had approached me right out of the blue, didn't know my name or anything. He was wearing a new, first-day-of-school, blue short-sleeved shirt and sneakers that showed a lot of playground mileage. "I'll give you a Milwaukee Braves bat if you can beat me" the skinny but strong

34

looking (in a wiry sort of way) kid wagered, confidently.

"OK" - and on the count of three we were racing before we even knew each other's names. I would come to realize that the new kid was a natural athlete; he also was the possessor of a pair of brass balls ("coglioni" grandpa would say) unlike anything I'd ever seen by seventh grade or since. I was not a natural athlete but I was pretty fast, faster than even I had realized. He had never been beaten in a footrace, until I got to the brick wall of our school a step and a half ahead of him that day. His surprise at losing was short-lived and he would, within a few days, deliver on his bold wager and hand me an official, game-used, Louisville Slugger bat. He told me his name was Dick Bellew but his friends call him Richie. How he got the bat and other Braves bats and balls, and even Eddie Matthews' glove, is a story all in itself, one that I would become a part of and benefit from as well; for now, suffice it to say, it was pretty much just a matter of not being afraid to ask. While that was my weakness, it was his strength and formed the basis for a close friendship that would last for the next eight years. Taking the rosin-stained bat from his hand, I said "Thanks, Richie". I would never call him by any other name.

That's how we met two years earlier. So, in 1959, Richie and I were carefully driving the go-kart along the sidewalk. My little brothers Mike and Mark were along too. We'd filled the gas tank up before we left home and knew we'd still have plenty left by the time we got to the grounds of the Wisconsin State Fair just a mile or so away. It was an early summer day and the fairgrounds would be empty since it was still weeks till Fair week would start. Earlier, we'd set up a little racing circle at the top of our driveway and we really whipped around that pretty darn fast. My other friends in the neighborhood, over on 88th Street, were all jealous; we were the only kids on the block who had one of these new go-karts. Now, it was on to the real racetrack at the State

Fair. I had it all figured out; if the State Fair cops or grounds-keepers ran into us, I'd tell them I was Mr. Mille's son, from Mille's Italian Sausage stand; they all knew him - grandma and grandpa too. We'd still get kicked out but probably nothing worse than that. Reaching the park, we were in luck; the 84th and Schlinger gate was wide open so we quickly entered the fairgrounds and moved along, watching out for trouble all the way. State Fair Park, when closed and totally empty of people, is always an eerie site and that day was no exception. On all sides, empty lots stood where the many food stands and other Fair attractions bustle during Fair week. As we moved along, the Coliseum and Dairy Building, as well as the empty livestock sheds, all helped to orient us. Of course, the grandstand of the mile racetrack itself, with its high, white-ish limestone wall was easy to see, even from a distance; its looming presence, surrounded by emptiness, only served to emphasize its importance as a shrine to American car racing. This had the effect of building on our excitement and gave us a sense of extreme privilege, however unearned it might be. With anticipation building, the edifice of the grandstand towering over us, and the entrance tunnel in our front, we simply rode right under the closed tunnel barrier (go-karts are pretty darn low) and, with the Briggs & Stratton lawn motor engine reverberating menacingly, shot down the echo chamber of the tunnel under the paved mile track. It was on this track here in the fairgrounds, that Roger Ward had been dominating the Indy-car ("big-cars", we called them) races for a few years. A.J. Foyt would win a couple of races here too, but that would be in the future. It had all gone well and we anticipated an exciting time trial on the famous "Paved Mile Track" of The Wisconsin State Fair, a track so famous that it would simply be referred to as "The Milwaukee Mile" in years to come. We'd decided earlier to start right there, on the famous mile track; we could do the inner sports car loop after that. I went first, being the *oldest brother and all. Starting in the pit area and, with Mark waving my red bandanna handkerchief [5], I floored the accelerator and was off onto the banked track.*

I can look back at many aspects of my life and recount experiences that exceeded my greatest expectations; winning the 220 yard dash in the state meet, my first real kiss, the births of my children - things like that. This was not among them. No. To cut right to the chase, there is nothing slower or more boring than going around a paved mile track at fifteen miles an hour. I guess if you put a lawn mower engine on a go-kart the thing will ride like a lawn mower, with a seat, and very low to the ground. I do know that, by the time I got all around that mile track the excitement had worn off for all of us. The banks of the track, steep for their day, were, in the vernacular of the Fair, like teats on a boar - useless and unnecessary and they only served to rub it in as I went slowly into the curves. Those unnecessarily banked turns made a good case for the power of gravity over centrifugal force. They taunted me for minutes but I did get a close-up look and the time to contemplate each and every crash point in those turns...red paint, yellow paint, blue - both light and dark - each paint remnant on the low concrete retaining wall memorialized the site of a crash, vestiges of real race cars with the length of the scrape suggesting the violence of the crash. After I finally completed the circuit, Richie got in the kart and opted for the sports car track that detoured from the mile oval to snake around the infield, promising a more racer-ly experience. It wasn't. Even the murderous hairpin at the south end of the track proved to be just a long, gradual turn more fit for watching scenery than a test of a young driver's courage. Such a disappointment. Forget about Roger Ward and

---

5   This was the bandanna that would embarrass mom when I would pull it out to blow my nose in fancy restaurants while complaining that I wanted to "be a cowboy" when I grew up and didn't want to wear those "stiff, dressy clothes."

Augie Pabst - we weren't even going as fast as Barnie Oldfield way back in nineteen o-nothing, not even close, but the name "Barnie" did feel somehow fitting for such a slow, boring ride.

We were never discovered by the State Fair authorities that day, unless perhaps, they saw us and just laughed and went back to work. Maybe, I don't know. But we did get back home with plenty of gas still in the tank and learned something about relativity. Not that any of us were Einsteins, certainly not me anyway, but we all came to the realization that a go-kart racing around a thirty foot driveway, at top speed, is going a lot faster than that same kart racing along a paved oval mile - at least in the way it matters.

SATURDAY 10:25 A.M.

After Robb and I rehash the glory years for a while (our times in the hundred and two-twenty get faster every time we see each other and I can't help but think that, if we live long enough, some Wisconsin state high school records will be broken.) I tell him that his hair is definitely grayer than mine and that he's got a face for radio but we both know he's better looking and we have some fun with it; all the while, I struggle to avoid making mistakes at the register, I'm that absorbed in our catch-up. Eventually, I promise to stop by his WOKY broadcasting site here on the fairgrounds, and after he leaves, I refocus on my register duties.

Les is cooking at the small stand today and that means I'll have someone to talk to about hunting and fishing. He's also a staunch Packer's fan (who here isn't?) and he will frequently test my allegiance to the green and gold now that I live in Philadelphia Eagles country. Although not necessary, I feel obligated to tell him that, while the Eagles are my adopted favorite right now, I have a real inner struggle each time the two teams meet. Attempting to garner his respect or, at least, appreciation, I point out that I donned my bright yellow cheese-head while eating wings and watching (pathetically, all by myself) the Pack play in the two recent Super Bowls of '96 and '97. He accepts this lame explanation but not the olive branch and disparages the Eagles every chance he gets. Les is one of Mikey's college buddies; he lives in the Neenah-Menasha area. His real name is Michael and he is Mike everywhere else - but at the Fair he's Les, a nickname derived from his last name. By now this probably does not require an explanation. A big man, he worked his way through school, laboring in the factories of the Fox River Valley where he learned to hold his own and had some interesting encounters. He has stories. Beer is one of Les's favorite pastimes but he also has a passion for big, sow-bellied walleyes and, since moving to lake-deprived eastern Pennsylvania years ago, I can't get my fill of ol' glasseye fishing tales. To top it off, he's also interested in military history which, while it's of interest to me now, will ultimately come back to bite me in the ass.

This young man in his late twenties or so is a marginal Mensa candidate (he says probably, I say maybe) and, though new on the job, he's already making suggestions for improving our operation. He points out things that I hadn't thought of though I've been staring at this grill for...I don't know...maybe fifty years? It's embarrassing, so I just mumble something about tradition and tell him to not burn the sausage. As if that's not annoying enough, he's also a young Republican and that creates a real problem for me - but the boy can cook! Yesterday he pulled a double shift without a break. Now, that may not mean much to most people, but having been one of the lead cooks myself for over twenty years, I am in awe. He stood next to a wall of flame on a ninety-degree day from

35 Cent Sandwich in the
1950s

Grandma and grandpa in the
old days

Tyler and new friends - Life is
good for a teen at the Fair

9:00 in the morning until midnight - the entire time handling spits so heavy with sausage they sometimes bend under the weight. That's never been done before. That's Mille's Hall of Fame kind of stuff. When I get a cook like that, I can put up with a whole lot of political differences.

Cooking on the Mille's grill is very different from any other form of charcoal grilling and it is not easy to learn (I was going to say "master" but, if truth be told, no one ever really masters it – if they're good, they just get reasonably comfortable with it and, upon getting to that point, the grill will humble them when they least expect it). Working the grill is much more of an art (there is a sort of Zen to it) than a science due to the many subtleties and uncontrollable variables that come into play. The fire is changing very rapidly and hot and cold spots need to be constantly identified and dealt with. Ash is accumulating, especially at the lower levels because, once loaded with charcoal in the morning, the cook continues to periodically add more throughout the day and night; it's simply poured on top of the live coals and, with the ashes falling through the bottom and sides of the grill, the old charcoal is displaced by the new. Ash builds up quickly and must be poked and shaken out ("shaking down the grill", we call it, and a messy chore it is!) or the fire will rapidly lose its heat; woe to the cook that allows that to happen during a rush period. Wind force and direction are also critical. Too much wind from the front of the grill will create tremendous heat and the spits must be turned constantly to avoid burning the sausage. Too little wind and it takes forever for new charcoal to ignite and provide the heat needed to get through a big dinnertime push.

With all this to deal with the cook must now handle anywhere from three to ten or more spits at a time, checking and turning them every minute or two. He has to constantly monitor demand to anticipate when the girls making sandwiches in the kitchen will need another spit - will it be in one minute or ten? Is the Fair crowd building up or dropping off? Are those thunderheads approaching (if it rains the crowd will run for cover and business will drop like a rock)? Who's playing in the grandstand tonight and what time does the show start (if it's a popular act the crowd will drop noticeably just before show time)? And so forth. Clearly, a cook at Mille's has his hands full.

To top it all off, the cook's also the star of the show; all eyes are on you when you're grilling. Make one slip and everyone sees it; dropping a full spit into the ash pit when 20 to 30 people are watching and waiting for you to finish off the sausages they're waiting for is, well, … embarrassing. At the same time however, if you're good, it's an opportunity to show-off by doing stuff like doubling-up (two spits in one hand), spinning (quickly rotating the spit with its tip balanced precariously in the notch of the rack), and assorted other spit-handling flourishes. A good cook tends to use these advanced techniques more frequently when attractive women are waiting and watching (or so my sister and brothers have pointed out to me).

1959

I never saw my grandfather, Amatore, move fast. Never. An Italian immigrant from Bari in the south of Italy, he was a man who was in permanent slow motion…always smelling the roses. He loved life, loved to have fun, and loved his grandchildren. Amo, amas, amat - I love, you love, he loves - Amatore.

Grandpa and my grandmother were poorly matched in an ar-

ranged marriage following the death of my natural grandfather in 1918 during the great flu epidemic. He wasn't the best mate for her but he was perfect for me. My siblings and I never knew our real grandfather but Amatore - grandpa - was the only one we ever needed. None of us ever thought of him as anything other than our real grandfather. I don't think we were even aware that he wasn't until we were no longer children. Even now, I sometimes forget that he was not a blood relation.

It's the summer of 1959. I'm 15 years old and on crutches having broken my right ankle during two-a-days with the Pius XI High School football team. With my sophomore season over before it started, I'm at the fairgrounds with grandpa and grandma and my little brother Mike, who's only eleven. The Fair starts in two days but our stand is set up in the wrong location, in a large open area just north of the Dairy Building and a bit southwest of the Lutheran Dining Hall. Dad has arranged for us to operate in a better spot down Second Street toward the grandstand, near the Pabst Beer Garden. But he's working at the new family restaurant, MichaelAngelo's, across town and it's just grandpa, grandma (who's off tending to other things), young Mike, and me - and I'm on crutches.

I come hobbling out of the screen door of the Lutheran Dining Hall and see grandpa walking toward our stand with a guy I can only describe as a cowboy. He's probably a roustabout with the Ringling Brothers Barnum and Bailey Circus (they're performing in the grandstand this year) but he's wearing something straight out of a cowboy movie - western hat, boots, cowboy shirt - he's got everything but the horse. As I crutch-hop my way to them, they stop at the stand.

The cowboy circles around the stand like he's looking over a used car to buy. Only thing is, he's selling, not buying. This lanky guy with the mother-of-pearl snaps on his shirt (no buttons for him!) is cocky and brash and is pitching to grandpa that, for a small fee, he can drag our already assembled stand all the way to our new spot on Second Street, thus avoiding the effort of knocking it down, transporting the sections, and reassembling it - all of which is work - and grandpa's strong suit is play, not work. He used to tell me that when he first came over from Italy (to escape the World War I draft, which probably sounded like a lot of effort to him) he worked for the railroad, laying rail. Now, if old family photos are to be believed, grandpa was a strong, well built young man, thick without being fat, and he certainly would have been capable of that sort of grunt work, but I pity the foreman who had to watch over him.

"Hell, nuthin' to it, I can do that in my sleep" the roustabout says with a smile that leaves me less than totally confident. But he's not talking to me.

"Quanto?" asks grandpa, with upraised salt and pepper brows that plead for a low fee, while rubbing his right thumb and index finger together in the universally understood reference to cash.

Like all of the State Fair knockdown concession structures, the stand is very flimsy and not meant to be moved once assembled. Consisting of simple frame sections held together by a few bolts and with no cross bracings to provide structural strength, it is unlikely to survive a parade across these open lots and down Second Street. This conversation is going in the wrong direction and, without waiting for the cowboy's response to grandpa's question, I hobble off to see if I can find grandma before something really bad happens.

Antonette Mille - grandma - could not be more different from grandpa. The only common characteristic they share is a loving, nurturing relationship with my siblings — Antoinette (with just an i added to grandma's name), Michael, Mark, - and me. An Italian immigrant, she survived and prospered in the face of difficulties that would have been insurmountable to many others. As a young woman, she left the small, hill village of Pomarico in the poor, rural, mountainous countryside of southern Italy and came to the U.S. She married a young man from the same village in Italy and, with the birth of Michael (my father), their future looked bright. This all changed when the great flu epidemic of 1918 struck. Spreading like the black plague throughout the world, few families were left untouched - in their case, it was her husband who was lost to this terrible virus. Other relatives felt that Antonette could not survive without a husband to support her. They obviously didn't know her very well or maybe it was just the times. In any case, they arranged a marriage between her and a gregarious young man, a widower, who also had come over from the old country. Amatore Mille was his name. He had a daughter, Irene, a few years older than Michael, who would pass away, tragically, soon after their marriage. From a practicality perspective, the marriage seemed to make sense for everyone involved, but it ignored the element of chemistry. They were not a good match. Grandma was stoic and industrious, a classic example of the immigrant who worked hard to get ahead in America, the land of unlimited opportunity. Grandpa was happy-go-lucky, more interested in small talk, kidding around, and reminiscing than in building a business and creating security. Beyond that basic incompatibility there may have been other problems as well but, if so, we children were shielded from it.

Rather than depend on the support of her newly assigned husband, Antonette began working as a seamstress in a Milwaukee garment factory where she quickly received the favorable attention of management and the opposite from her co-workers, as she exceeded all productivity standards. Re-assigned to the most difficult operation, the sewing of pockets, her income rose steadily and she invested most of what she earned, and she invested wisely. Real estate was her choice, more specifically, the purchase of rental income-generating small, single family homes on Milwaukee's south side, especially in the neighborhood of 10th Street just north of Mitchell Street. Never having had any sort of formal education, she quickly became self-educated, particularly in matters of business. Although unschooled, she knew and understood the difference between simple and compound interest and used her knowledge and instincts to her family's advantage.

An entrepreneurial drive pushed her to start the Italian sausage business, first at Italian street festivals in the 3rd Ward section of Milwaukee, then in 1932, when an acquaintance suggested it, at the Wisconsin State Fair. Dad was only 16 when they started at the Fair but he worked hard to support his mother's initiative and, as for grandpa, well, he helped too, when she could find him.

When dad married my mother, Alice, in 1941 they lived together with grandma and grandpa on 10th Street in one of grandma's houses. And her house (and home) it truly was, as mom was to realize and struggle with for many years, even now in 1959. Through the sheer strength of her personality, grandma has enforced her position as the matriarch of the family, even to the degree of forcing herself between my mother and me. I, consequently, have developed a very strong tie to my grandmother. For better or worse, that's just the way it is. The same is not true of my brothers and sister and that may be because I'm the oldest son - a special child in an Italian family. In any case, we are very close. At the dinner table, it is she I sit next to while my brother Mike sits next to our mother. As grandma reinforces my bad table manners, though not bad by Italian immigrant standards, mom slowly stews but lacks the power and support to usurp grandma's authority. Only many years later will I understand these family dynamics and attempt to come to terms with them. But that is in the future. For now, it is grandma that I seek.

After a short search I find her, with my little brother, on Second Street at the new location where we will be setting up. "Amatore, where-a you grampa?" she asks even before I can say anything. Her English is poor and her accent is just as thick as grandpa's even after being in this country for about fifty years. Always a stout woman, she is wearing one of her many similar housedresses, patterned with flowers - her only real passions were flowers and building security for her family - and, even in this heat, I know she is restrained by the heavy corset that I grew familiar with as a child, having felt its hard stiffness against my head as I lay on the sofa with my head in her lap.

"He's over by the stand. Did you talk to dad about moving it down here today? Did he say anything to you about moving the stand or when he's coming out here?"

"Non" she replies with a concerned, confused look on her dark complexioned face.

"Let's go see grandpa; come on." We start back to where I just came from but before we walk even twenty feet, encumbered as I am, we hear a strange, unfamiliar and out-of-place sound that gradually increases in volume and intensity. It's an ungodly noise; of wood scrapping heavily and mercilessly against concrete and gravel, screaming in agony as its fiber is being twisted and torn to the absolute breaking point. Looking in that direction, I see a 1949 or 1950 red Ford pick-up towing our sausage stand along Second Street toward us. The cowboy is at the steering wheel, left arm resting on the open door window, and he is no longer looking so damn confident or cocky. The smart-ass smile is off his face and he now looks like a guy who is worried about the reception he's going to get at the other end if this thing turns into so

many toothpicks. Grandpa, meanwhile, is walking alongside the stand frantically motioning for the cowboy to slow down as he notices the left side of the stand buckling in at the joint of two of its sections. Although still not exactly speedy, this is the fastest I have ever seen grandpa move.

"Ahh Marone!⁶" says grandma.

"Oh Christ!" I add.

But the cowboy continues on. The unnatural screeching and groaning sound is getting louder as he gets closer and closer. There is no turning back. Finally, the pickup and its load come to a stop in front of the new location. Quite a few people, considering the Fair is not yet open to the public, have gathered and we cautiously approach to assess the damage. Walking slowly around the stand, I notice a few cracks where there should not be cracks and the left side is still noticeably caved-in. The cowboy is now alongside and appears to be regaining his confidence...for no apparent reason. Grandma is saying something to grandpa in a very angry, loud tone; she is talking very fast and has reverted totally to Italian, as she is wont to do when excited. I am hearing Italian words and phrases that I have never heard before and which do not appear in any Italian-English dictionary. Grandpa is now talking back to her and both of them are now using their arms and hands, making gestures that, by their very nature, cannot be either friendly or conciliatory and, after a few moments of this, they finally walk away from each other.

"This'll straighten right out" proclaims the cowboy, kicking at the crease in the frame with his well-worn black boots. "Where do you want it?" he asks. "Just have to move my ropes and I'll slide it right in,

---

6   "Marone" is, in the southern Italian dialect, literally "Madonna" - as in the blessed Virgin - but its meaning is somewhat lost in translation. Better to think of it as being more equivalent to an emphatic "SweetJesusMaryJoseph!"

48

good as new." *Slowly, I begin to realize that, all things considered, the stand has withstood the cruel assault pretty well. Grandma has begun to cool down and her flushed-face is returning to its natural dusky complexion. Grandpa is recovering from her attack and is now showing his hired hand where he wants the stand to sit. Pent-up emotion is a concept that is just as foreign to grandma and grandpa as is the English language itself. After a few more minutes, the stand has been pulled into its assigned space, but is not perfectly aligned and certainly not plumb. Tex, or whatever his name is, has walked over after retrieving something big and heavy looking from the bed of the pick-up; it hangs from his hand but his leg conceals it from my view as he walks into the stand. I hop after him with a new sense of dread.*

"All this sumbitch needs is a BFH adjustment of about 5 degrees and it'll be perfect" he says to me while looking at the stoved-in sections on the left side.

"What's a BFH?" I naively ask, still leery of his intent.

"Big friggin' hammer" he replies under his breath (only he uses a much stronger word than "friggin"), nodding at his big sledge hammer with a vulgar smile meant just for me, all the time being careful that grandma is out of earshot. I'm not sure if he's trying to be a gentleman in the presence of a woman or just wants to avoid the sort of shit-storm he just saw her lay on grandpa. In any case, he lifts the long handled sledgehammer and proceeds to whack at the side of the stand. WHOMP ...WHOMP.... He steps back and admires his fine adjustment while I walk around the perimeter picking up a few splinters and assessing the stand's overall condition.

His handiwork done, the Man From The West and grandpa light the unfiltered Camels that grandpa has offered and are walking off together to finish their transaction and perhaps...no, probably...celebrate its success over a Schlitz or maybe even a glass of his homemade red wine.[7] *Grandma is recovered and is beginning to move supplies into the stand; Mike walks (and I hobble) in to help her.*

In years to come the Fair administrators, in one aspect of a major fairgrounds improvements program, will approach dad and ask him to make a big financial investment by becoming the first food concessionaire to construct a permanent structure on the fairgrounds. After careful consideration, he will agree to the proposal and the knock-down Mille's stand will be replaced by an attractive and efficient permanent building, just a bit further away on Second Street. But, for a number of years, every time I look at a certain ding in the wooden frame of this stand, one that approximates the shape of the face of a sledgehammer, I will remember grandpa and the cowboy.

7   Italy is home to many excellent red wines - Barolo, Chianti Classico, the aptly named Vino Nobile, and, arguably the noblest of all, Brunello di Montalcino. Grandpa's "dego red" - and let me just say that as an Italian myself, I take no offense at this ethnic appellation - would never be confused with any of these great wines - nor even those of the next lower tier, or the next. No, his wine, home-made from the Muscat grapes of California's Turano Brothers, was the wine of southern Italian peasants and, what it lacked in quality, he made up for in quantity. Although not one who drank to excess, he was never far from a gallon jug of his home-pressed wine and it would not surprise me if he had packed-in a gallon jug with the other essential State Fair supplies.

CHAPTER 3

TONI AND THE
LITTLE THEATRE

SATURDAY 11:30 A.M.

EVERYTHING IS UNDER CONTROL IN THE KITCHEN HERE IN THE
small stand and Les is keeping up with the growing crowd. We
have lots of time on our hands during these long days and the
conversation can go off in unusual, trivial directions. He and I just
had a debate about the best type of socks to wear with sneakers;
actually, this is not trivial and is a real dilemma - I'm coming off a
lifetime of knee-high Wigwams that have slowly evolved (survival
of the species not being a dominant trait of elastic) into slouch
socks, all accordioned-up at my ankles...which my wife says look
like ballet leg warmers. Finally ready to take the plunge into either
ankle high or sneaker-top high ("no-show", if you will) alterna-
tives, I ask Les for his opinion and soon wish I hadn't. He makes
it clear that if I show up with footlets on my feet he will find a
way to sew pink pom-poms on them. This is not an idle threat

and I take it very seriously. He himself is old-school and wears mid calf cotton sweat socks; manly, yes, but dated. It occurs to me that you can probably line up a bunch of sneakered guys in shorts behind a knee-high screen and guess their relative ages just by the socks they wear. It's kind of like the hair-thing where a guy (many women, too) will continue to wear the hairstyle they had in their peak years for the rest of their lives…and even, through the efforts of well-trained morticians, to the eternal hereafter. How else do you explain the hairstyles you see on some people? Thinking about this far more than it deserves, I finally decide I'll take my chances tomorrow with ankle high socks and then I tell Tyler to wait on the man at the other end of the counter, the older gentleman with the mullet.

Old friends and acquaintances know where to find us during the Fair, so we see quite a few, and that's a great part of being here every year. Already, today, I've seen a couple of old friends from my Milwaukee days; I immediately know the era when they call out my name. If it's "Hey Amatore" I know it's probably a St. Anthony of Padua elementary school acquaintance or possibly someone from my Pius XI High School days. On the other hand, if it's a "Hi Matt" I can be pretty assured that, when I turn to acknowledge the voice, it will be someone from either the University of Wisconsin-Milwaukee or from life after college, perhaps someone from Milwaukee's A.O. Corporation where I worked for twelve years right after graduating from college. One of the "Amatore"s earlier today turned out to be an old friend who was a St. Anthony's schoolmate. He was surprised when I immediately recognized him after all these years and we talked about the old days in seventh and eighth grade. Waxing nostalgic, I shared with him the secret crush I had on Margaret Kreuger during those years. He got a huge kick out of that and admitted having had the same secret infatuation - which should not have been a surprise to me, but it was and I enjoyed the revelation.[8]

LATE 1970S

The sun is unbearable on this dog-day afternoon but that old expression will soon have a new meaning for me. It's extremely hot and I'm cooking at the big stand. Dad walks over to the counter and strikes up a conversation with a guy I recognize. He's the young fellow in the brown leather jacket who rides the Harley Davidson in the daily parade around the fairgrounds. That's nothing special, not even here in Milwaukee, Harley's home, but the twist that makes this biker parade-worthy is the dog. How often, one must ask, do you see a real dog sitting on the two-up passenger seat of a motorcycle, her hands...I mean, paws...resting on the shoulders of the driver? They ride around the fairgrounds in the parade like that. The canine even wears goggles, which are a nice, if unnecessary, touch. The brownish dog is some type of mixed breed, so muddled, in fact, that I can't make out any dominant features that would suggest its ancestry, save, perhaps, the slightest suggestion of German shepherd in her distant family tree. This lack of pedigree seems appropriate; it just wouldn't be fitting for a Harley dude to be seen riding with a Bichon Frise or a King Charles spaniel,

---

8   Margaret (Krueger was not her real name) with her shoulder length blond page-boy hair, was attractive and very mature, physically, for her age, particularly so for that era. I, on the other hand, was extremely shy and scared to death of girls, but I liked them. I can vividly, still now, remember her turning at her desk in front of me to hand me a stack of assignment papers. The mysterious shape of her left breast pressing against her tight, fuzzy yellow sweater was almost too much to take. By today's standards, this probably doesn't seem like much but, in 1957, for a shy thirteen-year old boy in the eighth grade of St Anthony of Padua ...it was enough.

at least not here in Milwaukee, at the State Fair. *Dad is still talking to this guy and he seems to have something in mind as I hear him tell the kitchen girls to wrap up a sandwich with extra peppers, then hands it to the young man, complements of Mille's. They carry on their conversation as I wonder what the deal is, but then get wrapped up in topping off my charcoal.*

Later, things are not particularly busy and dad is sitting at the beer tap occasionally pouring a brew whenever one of the wait-staff shouts out an order. Over to my left, my brother Mike is at the register and Mark is on a lunch break. Looking at dad, I wonder when his appearance began to change; in old family photos he bore a striking resemblance to the actor Al Pacino who, not many years ago, got a lot of acclaim in the movie, The Godfather but now he looks a lot like Humphrey Bogart, at least I think he does. I hope I age as well as he has.

"Hey Mr. Mille, How ya doin'?" a voice calls out.

Turning to look, I see a middle-aged man, who I don't recognize, approach the counter while smiling at dad. He's wearing a white, short sleeved, dress shirt, which is probably an oxymoron but that's what he's wearing. He's also got a pocket protector with a couple of pens in it.

"How have you been, young man?" dad replies with a friendly but somewhat less than totally warm smile.

Slowly, as if hinting of reluctance, he eases himself off the stool at the tap and steps to the counter. Shaking hands with the guy (who now has the broad smile of someone who has just run into a dear old friend in dad), my father and he begin a conversation that I cannot hear. This continues for ten minutes and I'm now curious, wondering who the fellow is. I walk past the two of them, feigning a bored cook's random stroll, but I still can't pick out anything that helps me to identify who dad's friend is. I give up and after a few minutes more the guy leaves to a hearty handshake.

*I'm really curious now and walk up to dad, close to his ear.
"Dad, who was that guy?" I ask softly, just in case it's some kind
of secret.*

*"I have NO idea..." he says with an emphasis on the NO, a sly
grin on his face and his voice low...cautious, should the guy still be
in earshot. Shaking my head in amused surprise, I counter his grin
with one of my own and am amazed that he just had a ten minute
conversation with a total stranger (to him) and made the guy feel like
he was an old friend. I'm pretty sure I would not be able to pull that off.
I also now know that whenever I hear a "How have you been, young
man?"(The "young man" part is the tip-off) from dad, there's a good
chance he has no idea who he's talking to.*

*I gained a new respect for my father's people-skills that day. As
a prominent restaurateur, he is well known by many people, most of
whom have met him only briefly and, often, a number of years in the
past and in any number of contexts. Dad, on the other hand, is sitting
in a popular food concession that has his name on the sign and, in
case anyone missed that, his name is also on his shirt. It seems like an
unfair situation – people should have to wear nametags if they're going
to expect him to know who they are when they approach him like that
– but, on the other hand, he handles himself just fine.*

*Late afternoon, and it's hotter than ever. Anxious looking high
school kids in colorful, brutally heavy, marching band uniforms, better suited to October football, stand at attention awaiting their cue.
They're directly in front of us here at the big stand on Second Street.
Assistants scurry around them, spraying a cooling mist in their faces to
counter the scorching heat. They need to keep the kids' body tempera-
tures down. One of the plume-crested drummers strikes a cadence and,
all at once, the horns join in as the familiar rhythm of ON WISCONSIN
is suggested, if one listens carefully. Proud parents, smiling broadly as*

if looking into a maternity ward window, are easily picked out from among the crowd that's lined up on both sides of Second Street. The "mist-ers" pick up their own pace now, running here and there, adding tiny water droplets to the eyeglasses of a skinny tuba player (isn't it a requirement that they be chubby?) who had seemed to struggle with the sheet music even under better conditions. Never mind all that, the kids really do pretty well, as young as they are, and in this oppressive heat. The rendition ends and the band marches on to the drummers beat. In front and behind them are a variety of marching bands, extraordinary vehicles, and menageries, including draft horses pulling fancy wagons, among them the curiously-welcomed Anheuser Busch Clydesdales of St. Louis - them, again - (how come Milwaukee's own Miller of "The Champagne of Bottled Beer" fame doesn't have a wagon, pulled preferably by Percherons?). The parade is in full swing! As the mixed-procession continues to stream past the front of the stand I notice that dad, with his well-receded hairline covered by his Wisconsin State Fair cap, is smiling and looking back along the oncoming parade route in seeming anticipation. Why? He's been out here for something like forty years now with a parade coming past most every day. Yet, he still seems intrigued. This strikes me as interesting. Then, as the parade progresses, I understand. There, now right in front of our stand, slowing down, revving his engine, and waving to us as he goes by, is the brown-jacketed Harley rider. He's always in the parade, of course, but today his passenger, the canine of Heinz 57 varieties, is proudly (if I can say that of a dog) wearing a "Mille's Italian Sausage — Since 1932" T-shirt. We, all of us in the stand, cheer loudly, both for him and for dad, who has pulled off an advertising coup - at the cost of a sausage sandwich with extra peppers. He'll be in a very good mood all the rest of the day, and maybe even into tomorrow morning.

Later, I'm sitting at the beer tap eating my fourth sandwich of the day. It's a combo with both sweet and sharp peppers, and it tastes just as good as the first. The sausage juice is messy and so are my hands. Noticing me wolfing down the sandwich, dad, who's now at the register, gives me a slight, knowing-grin and slowly nods his head up and down in acknowledgement. No one other than family members would pick-up on his subtle gesture, but I know exactly what he is communicating. His reaction is one of pride and stems from knowing that his product is considered by many to be the best sandwich at the Fair. Every day we will have customers walk up to us and tell us that Mille's is always their first stop at the Fair. Every day.[9]

"Dad, wouldn't it be something if we could take this across the country, to the major fairs" I ask, more as a statement of fact than as a question.

"The Royal American people tried to get me to do that years ago" he replies, referencing the carnival that has the Fair midway contract. "You get sawdust in your veins in that business" he adds in a dismissive tone but there is something about the distant look in his eyes and the way he says it that suggests a certain regret. It's subtle, but it's there. I read into it an imagined might-have-been, a regret of not being able to chase a bigger dream, showing the entire country what he has built by taking chances, working hard, and never compromising on quality. It is a dream that, in a few years, I will seriously consider pur-

---

9 Many years later, in 2005, when sitting at the register of the small stand, I will see Jim Doyle, the Governor of Wisconsin, approaching the employee's entrance to the cream puff operation in the Dairy Building. I knew he would be coming because his handlers have been milling about, communicating on walkie-talkies, for a couple of hours. As his entourage approaches, he suddenly veers off and walks over to our stand. His people look a bit alarmed and unprepared to deal with his spontaneous diversion and quickly scurry after him. He extends his hand to me, introduces himself, and tells me that his kids are always telling him "Mille's is their favorite stop at the Fair".

suing myself and, in so doing, eventually realize what Mille's Italian Sausage is really all about. It will be a hard but life changing lesson. It will also bring an important revelation to me, one that will result in a greater appreciation of my father than I could have ever imagined.

1950s

    It was interesting but mysteriously out of place...a professional microscope, all black with shiny brass fixtures at its turret-like head... heavy, very heavy, with two small wooden boxes containing glass slides, each with a cloudy blur of varying colors and tints...each with a cryptic handwritten label. We found it in our basement while playing down there. Our home was not the sort of place where you would expect to find a professional-quality Bausch and Lomb microscope, but there it was, surrounded by boxes of soda cups, long shelves supporting dozens of gallon jars of home-preserved sharp peppers, and a variety of other restaurant supplies. Its presence there was just as incongruent as would be the finding of a sheet-covered pile of restaurant equipment in the attic of a family with a long tradition of careers in science...and it just made us kids wonder.

    We played with it; how could we not? If we managed to adjust the focus just right, the blurred slide seen through the eyepiece would suddenly become a clear image, but of what we still didn't know. Many years later, this microscope's presence in our home will be understood and will help me to clearly see my father's relationship with his immigrant mother...and how, through different perspectives, both really wanted the same thing after all.

Mille's stand in front of The Little Theatre a long time ago

Mike, mom, and Mark guarding the till in 1967

Donna and Mary making sandwiches

SATURDAY 12:45 P.M.

The state inspector has decided to make an unannounced visit to check out our operation, here at the small stand, today. They are always unannounced - but, as always, that's a non-event for us. He's walking around the kitchen and the back storage room, thermometer in hand and clipboard at his side. The kitchen staff has been drilled from the first morning by Toni and they all know the importance of complying with the State codes associated with all food preparation businesses. Counter tops are constantly being washed. Hats and food handling gloves are in place (although the hat part is always a battle with the teenage girls), trash is quickly removed from the kitchen, and so forth.

Just as within our own family, several generations of Wisconsin state health inspectors have also come and gone. The last two to retire on us still come around from time to time as customers, just to say hi and see how everyone's doing. Both of them, and the other inspectors, have often commented on how our operation is a model that they refer to when dealing with others - at the State Fair and elsewhere. It is a nice complement but, more importantly, we never have to worry about being shut down, not because of any favoritism but because Toni is keeping things up to code here in the small stand and my sisters-in-law, Mary and Donna, are doing the same over at the big stand.

The cell phone that we use to keep in touch with the big stand suddenly chimes. I answer it on the third ring.

"Yeah?"

"Hi -This is Mille's on Second" a male voice says. The background noise makes it difficult to hear but I recognize that it's Mike. He goes on "we're having a problem with our Coke lines and need service."

I pause for a moment before realizing that my brother thinks he's called the Coca Cola State Fair service phone number but, obviously, did one of those cell phone redial-things and got us by mistake.

"Who'd you say this is?" I reply in the gruffest voice I can muster.

"Mille's on Second; we need service right away."

"Well, it's gonna be awhile."

"What do you mean?" a nervous and slightly annoyed voice replies.

"We're all jammed up; we've got some priority customers we have to take care of today. We can probably get to you first thing tomorrow."

There's a slight pause while my incredulous and now very annoyed brother processes what he just heard. It's a response he's never heard before, at least not stated so blatantly.

"We can't wait till tomorrow...we have customers...what are we supposed to do...just shut down?" (At this point, I can almost feel the heat through the phone) "We aren't able to serve...Who IS this?..........Is that YOU Matt?"

He hears me chuckle.

"You son of a bitch; I thought I was dialing Coke."

"Yeah, I know. Gotcha!" Mike throws some good-natured insults my way and we hang up.

1978

Southfield, Michigan lies just outside of Detroit in its northwest suburbs; I've been living here since leaving Wisconsin in 1976 and I'm sitting at my desk at work. A just-completed handwritten letter to my father, dated August 29, 1978, sits in front of me. It's early evening and there are empty offices all around; they've been empty all day. Deeply frustrated with my twelve year career in information technology, I look at the letter and at the vacant offices. My associates and I have worked hard to build a significant business but now many of them are being terminated - laid-off is too nice of a euphemism - or are departing of their own accord due to a major re-direction in my employer's market focus. I've decided it's time for me, too, to make a change. I feel a driving need to get some control back into my career and the only way to accomplish that, it seems, is to start my own business.

The timing of my decision has been affected by other, related events. Just about a week ago, my family and I completed yet another very successful run at the Wisconsin State Fair. We worked hard, together, for eleven days, had a record year...and had fun doing it. As always, we received many complements on a daily basis as well as constant expressions of curiosity and interest in the unique Mille's charcoal grill. This has goaded me to stop being passive and actually do something.

Why not? If we can do so well in Milwaukee, why not take the business to other major fairs across the U.S. - hell, all of North America for that matter. Not only could I gain some control over things, I could also be working in a positive, enjoyable environment, a situation I've always thrived in. There's every reason to believe that, over time, Mille's Italian Sausage, with our unique grill, can be a big hit all across the country. My letter to dad explains my frustration and strong desire to do something to help myself and my family – my wife and three children. It speaks of the opportunity at hand. It seizes the imagination of a man, my father, who for years has wondered…what if?

I complete the letter and sign it – and leave it on my desk. The letter will never be mailed.

1954

"Amatore – go get your sister" dad shouts out to me from the cash register.

"OK dad."

I pull my arms from the big metal Schlitz Beer cooler chest where I've been fishing-out pieces of a broken beer bottle. I've only been working at it for a few minutes but I welcome the break from the frigid water; my arms are soaked and pink from the cold but they'll warm up quickly. It's a small price to pay for the privilege of also doing the fun part, chopping up the big blocks of ice with the ice pick, the one with the wooden handle and the Coca Cola trademark printed on it in red. This same ice pick will provide hours of fun for my brother Mike and me when we use it to play a game something like mumbly peg that we call "stretch" on the grass behind the stand. I'm ten years old this year and the State Fair is a world of constant wonders.

The 4H Club Band is performing just on the other side of the Police Department Building from our stand, each kid dressed all in white with military-style little white caps. Across the street and catty-corner from us at the corner of Grandstand Avenue and Main Street is the sweeping curved front of the Miller High Life concession. Up high, the striking image of a smiling, attractive woman with a tall, som-brero-style hat and a short, flaring skirt sits on a crescent moon and beckons thirsty men and women - but mostly the men. The champagne of bottled beer. In sharp contrast to this and within a few yards of it is the "All You Can Drink - Milk 10 Cents" stand with its stylized min-iature dairy cows stabled along the roof line, just in case you can't read. Imagine, at this single intersection a fairgoer of any age can sample Milwaukee's AND Wisconsin's Finest!

I know where to find Toni; we all know where to find Toni. I hop on the counter and drop to the grass outside the stand where mom is taking a break sitting on a folding chair while my little six-year old brother Mike plays with a toy cap gun - a recent purchase from one of the Fair vendors. He wants to ride the ponies again and mom will likely take him there later.

"Where are you going?" she asks.

"Dad wants Toni."

I pretend to be playing football. I'm a running back cutting back and forth through the crowd, using my blockers wisely, and complete the short fifteen yard effort as I get to the end zone, the high, arcing entrance to The Little Theatre.

Although I know just about every square foot of this theatre, which is used for amateur performances, it is an alien world to me. Not so, for Toni. When walking through its huge doors she enters a world that pulls at her soul. Sitting and watching and internally acting out each female role that is portrayed on stage, she is in a place where she was meant to be. At home, she stages her own plays. With the two-car ga-rage as the stage, the rising curtain (the garage door) will open on her productions. Years later, our neighbor will tell us how they watched her plays, in amusement, from their kitchen window. Toni gives our little brother Mark, who is only four, the roles that Mike and I refuse. We have reached the age of consent, he has not, but neither has he reached the age of non-consent...so Toni makes the decision for him. And so, with full cast, it's lights, camera, action.[10]

But at this moment, here at the Fair, my sister is simply enraptured by the performance on stage and I have to bring her back to the here and now. Finding her in the usual seat, I say, a bit too loudly and inconsiderately, "Toni - Dad wants you."

"What does he want?" she whispers without taking her eyes off the stage.

"I don't know; I think he's taking a break."

My sister is always reluctant to leave The Little Theatre during a performance but she is now anticipating the possibility of a special opportunity with dad. Returning to the stand with me, she approaches dad. He sees us and ducks under the counter to join us outside the stand; mom, with her black and white Bakelite elliptical shaped sunglasses, has taken his place at the register. Grandma is working silently inside the stand, her five foot four inch stout figure fills her sleeveless housedress and her presence dominates the kitchen area. Her hair is beginning to gray but is still mostly dark and thick and her hands move quickly...the

---

10 The "camera" part was occasionally provided by dad. Never much of a photographer, he had resorted to the use of an amazing stereoscopic 3D camera. So foolproof was this camera that even his color photos, which were projected and viewed while wearing 3D glasses, just like in the movies, would draw oooh's and aaah's every time. Composition? Not an issue; the extra dimension - depth - provided by the camera more then offset any artistic shortcomings of the photographer. It was the equivalent of putting a fifty-inch plasma high-def TV into 1950s homes that had never seen anything but 12" black and white television. Even today, when people view these well-preserved slides they are in awe. Those old images of me, a geeky-looking, skinny kid in 1950s era cowboy shirts and a perpetual cowlick, still draw hearty laughs, especially in 3D...as if two dimensions of humiliation weren't enough!

bread knife making sure, rapid cuts into the long loaves of French bread that dad brought in this morning from Gardetto's Bakery. Grandpa, in his old brown shoes and prematurely silvered hair stands outside of the stand, leaning on the counter, smoking a Camel and talking with a customer. His eyes occasionally move to the grill in an act of passive supervision. Both of them, grandma and grandpa, smile warmly at Toni and me as we approach dad. Angelo Marco is manning the grill; he's dad's close friend and future partner in a very upscale Italian supper club, which will conveniently be named MichaelAngelo's. Late last night, I watched as Angelo had quickly jumped onto the counter at the front corner of the stand, that corner nearest the Miller High Life concession across the street. He rushed to pour a bucket of water that he scooped from the beer cooler onto the flames that had flared up after a burning remnant of the evenings fireworks drifted onto our canvas roof. We kids always look forward to the fireworks at the end of the grandstand show but last nights were really exciting!

"Where have you been Antoinette? Do you want to go dancing or not?" dad says with a smile.

"Really? Can we go now? Mom, dad's going to take me to the Modernistic!" she proclaims excitedly. Mom smiles as my sister and father leave the stand and walk to the Modernistic Ballroom. There, dad and Toni will practice the dances that he and mom enjoyed during the big band era which is now on its last legs. They will also practice the popular new dances. The mambo is all the craze. They will dance to the big hit of Rosemary Clooney, MAMBO ITALIANO. Not to be outdone, Perry Como has released PAPA LOVES MAMBO and they will dance to it as well.

There is another new trend in music – embodied by a guy named Bill Haley with "His Comets" – who has a song titled SHAKE, RATTLE AND ROLL that is now very popular with teenagers. My sister will find herself situated squarely on the cusp of the music of an earlier era and this new style that is being referred to as "rock and roll" by some disc jockeys. While most of her friends at school embrace the rebellious new form, she has no such leanings and will retain a passion for the popular and classical music of the pre-rock era. She will watch, repeatedly, every MGM musical made in the 40's and 50's. Gene Kelly, Jeanette MacDonald, Fred Astaire, and the great Enrico Caruso - these are the names she knows and admires. Her passion for this music and the stage itself, kindled while sitting in The Little Theatre, will become a driving force in her life. In one of those fortunate conjunctions of aspiration and ability, she will follow her bliss until one day, far in her future, she will fondly look back at The Little Theatre from center stage of a larger theatre - a much larger theatre.

GRANDPA'S
SECRET TROUT FLY

SATURDAY 2:10 P.M.

BRIAN IS WORKING AT THE BIG STAND. HE'S COOKING WITH ROY and doing some sausage spitting[11] as well. Yet another of Mikey's college buddies, Brian is a high school teacher who takes advantage of his summer breaks to help us out at the Fair. He, like Roy, has been doing this for quite a few years. I'm back at the big stand myself just taking a break and visiting with the folks here. Brian slips the neck strap of his long green bib apron over his sandy-

---

11   Mille's sausage is seldom "spit" in the common usage of the word. Sausage spitting refers to the critical process of skewering the Italian sausages uniformly and tightly on the long steel spits. If not done properly, the cook will find himself working with a "spinner", meaning the sausages do not remain tightly packed but, rather, spin into various positions making that particular spit nearly impossible to handle and grill uniformly. One spinner can be forgiven…more then one will result in certain confrontation between cook and spitter. Brian is both master spitter and cook; spinners are not an issue for him.

haired head and reaches around to grasp the strings from behind, bringing them together in the front and tying them at the waist. "Man, this apron's getting tight" he says…to no one in particular. Big mistake…rookie mistake. Mark, sitting at the beer tap occasionally pouring as orders are called out, looks at me with an almost imperceptible, ever-so-slight grin - actually, more of a slight gleam in the eye accompanied by the slight raising of an eyebrow. It says to me "did you just hear that? We're about to have some fun!"

Brian is an interesting, hard working and good-looking guy but he's, well…stocky. If he were a girl, his mother would describe him as being big-boned. But he's not a girl - he's just a big, husky guy. He has huge, muscular calves; he thinks they're his best feature and is known to push the shorts season well into the winter months which, in Wisconsin, is really pushing it. The long apron, ending as it does just above the knees, accents his lower legs, which is probably why he's usually wearing his apron…maybe even why he agrees to work so hard during his summer teacher's break. We humor him whenever he flexes his calves and carries on about them. As for me, I just see two Easter hams with shoes and, if the truth be told, when he looks at those freckled[12] calves in the mirror (we know he does) that's probably what he sees as well, for Brian loves to eat - and there's a lot to eat at the Wisconsin State Fair - hence, his problem with the apron getting tight. On a typical day Brian has available to him fresh cannolis from our stand, huevos rancheros from the Mexican joint under the grandstand, ribs from Saz's down the street, black angus rib-eye steak sandwiches from the Cattleman's stand, baked potatoes, cream puffs, and on and

---

12 Cloves?

on - and, of course, Mille's Italian Sausage. As a special treat, he will have a choice of several dozen terrific Wisconsin-based microbrewery products (Spotted Cow is his current favorite). Brian also brings a lot of food from home, so much that we tease him about taking up an entire shelf ("Brian's Shelf") of our limited refrigerator space.

As Brian finally snugs the strings of his apron, my mind wanders as I contemplate what Mark may have up his sleeve. Rest assured, it will be good. I like to contrast the artistic (he is an artist, after all), clever, and subtle pranks of Mark to the approach that Les takes. Les's jokes and pranks are always on a grand scale; Herculean - he's the Cecil B. DeMille of prankdom. Once, a friend of his back in Appleton went away for a few days. After getting a key to the guy's flat from an accomplice, he proceeded to remove the entire interior doorway to the bedroom and dry-walled over where the doorway had been. He then painted that entire wall and hung a painting you-know-where. I would have paid to see his former friend's reaction upon returning home. It had to be something like a Twilight Zone moment. Les, of course, had to reverse-engineer all of his carpentry, probably while under a good deal of pressure. Les likes big pranks.

I'm back at the small stand again; Roy has switched with Les and is cooking here. Earphones on, he is listening to some classic Neil Young. His voice-over disguises the song but I soon recognize the familiar lyrics that speak of barkers and colored balloons and go on with:

> "It's so noisy at the fair, but all your friends are there, and
> the candy floss you had, and your mother and your dad"

"Roy, put a spit up front; we need a little flash" I say only to have to repeat myself, louder. Finally, flipping off the earphones and hearing me, Roy understands and quickly moves a spit from the back to the front and, without having to be told, up high.

1978

It's a month since I wrote the letter to my father. It remains, un-mailed, on my desk at work and it's now September. But my conviction remains strong and, finally, rather than mailing it, I just call dad and lay it all out. As I expected, he is intrigued by the possibilities. By the end of the call, we've agreed to a serious investigation of the venture…and so, my journey of discovery begins.

With a passion unmatched by anything I've done in my career to date, I throw myself into the planning and promotion of a new business venture – Mille's Italian Sausage operating at large fairs and festivals all across North America. The tasks involved seem myriad. There is equipment to be designed and built, market research to be conducted, suppliers to be lined up, marketing materials to be developed and produced, financing to be secured, and, most critically, venues to be sold and locked-in. The food concession business is extremely competitive and all major fairs are constantly barraged by hopeful vendors. The vast majority are politely turned away. Realizing this, I use my sales and marketing experience to put together a pitch that focuses on the attractiveness of our unique grilling technique (dad's "flash" factor) along with the long-term success and popularity of Mille's at the Wisconsin State Fair, one of the most highly regarded fairs in the entire country.

The response from various directors and concession managers of prestigious fairs across North America is, as hoped, quite positive. I am able to lock in contracts with the biggest venues in California, Arizona, Massachusetts, New York, Ontario, and Alberta. With contracts in hand, it is now possible for dad and me to secure financing from a local bank. This is quickly accomplished. Dad and I then fly to South Fulton, a small town in Tennessee where we spend most of the day with a company that specializes in the manufacture of mobile food concession trailers. It goes well and on our return trip, while waiting for our connecting flight in St. Louis, I watch as an Air Force jet takes off from a military runway and swoops into a seemingly impossible and breathtaking near-vertical climb, underscoring my own optimism.

Within a matter of a few weeks, our design of the mobile unit is finalized and its manufacture is begun. We also purchase a used refrigerated truck which will transport us and the sausage supply as well as haul the large sausage wagon. The last detail is the hiring of an assistant who will travel with me and help with the operation. Chuck, an old acquaintance of dad's is hired and, in the early spring of 1979 we load the truck with a fresh supply of sausage and depart for our first fair in Tucson, Arizona. On the way, we will make a stop in Tennessee to rendezvous with our new, shiny green sausage wagon.

1950s

As children, State Fair Park was our summer camp. Although we all helped run the business in ways that varied with our individual ages and inclinations, we also had lots of free time. For more than a week, every year, we had many free hours to explore the fairgrounds' varied aspects - its wooded picnic hill to the south of Honey Creek, the harness racing horse stables at the southeast corner of the park, the old coliseum with its vaulted ceiling. We - Toni, Michael, Mark, and I - each had our personal favorite spots and attractions. For me, as a young boy, it was the lure of the Indian mound at the Department of Natural Resources Exhibit that fired my imagination. Often, my eyes naively scanned its eroded sides hoping to spot the edge of an exposed pot or arrowhead. None was ever found but the ember that was fanned, there at that mound, would grow over the years and I would eventually, as a young man still obsessed with the hunt, find hundreds of arrowheads in the plowed fields surrounding Horicon Marsh and other such sites.

My sex education began at the State Fair, right there in the Penny Arcade. With the cranking of the handle of the Mutoscope, photo cards would flick one after another in rapid succession, creating a primitive movie effect; "real moving pictures" read the sign atop the ornate, cast iron machine. As I looked into the viewing mechanism (it's very design, peephole-like, promised illicit scenes inside) the flicking cards revealed a barely-clad female, albeit a bit on the portly side even by 1950s standards, going through a suggestive dance routine while holding a large rubber ball - for artistic merit. Before committing my coin to the slot, since the machine I was about to use had the hard-to-not-notice title of Red Hot Mamma plastered on its advertising poster, I would always check to see who was standing around...who might recognize me. After a casual (or so I hoped) glance around, if the coast was clear, I dropped my coin in the slot and quickly buried my face in the viewing scope which, for me, doubled as a mask. Now, having securely hidden my identity, ostrich-like, I was safe to relax and enjoy the moving-pictures show; never mind the fact that the name "MILLE" was written in large red - check that - scarlet, script letters across the back of my Italian Sausage T-shirt. In reality, the machine never delivered as much as it promised, no matter how many times I watched it or how adept I became at stopping the flicking cards at just the right point. So, at the end of the day, Red Hot Mamma still couldn't begin to take the place of Margaret Kreuger in my private thoughts.

Directly across the aisle from the Mutoscope was a punching bag with a meter that claimed to gauge how hard the bag had been hit. Here, teen-age delinquent-types with greasy ducktail haircuts ("D. A."s) and packs of cigarettes rolled up in their white T-shirt sleeves would rear back and hit the leather bag with everything they had, a very distracting sound to someone trying to concentrate. Other muscle men hung out at the Ring the Bell strength-game near the 84th Street gate. The over-sized operator's Harley was always parked inside his space and it was impressive to watch big-chested men swing the heavy mallet to catapult the metal clanger up the towering track to its hoped-for destiny with the bell. I developed such awe of those few men who could make the bell clang that, even in later years when I might have been able to accomplish the near-impossible myself, or at least come close, I would never even attempt it.

In the early years the Fair provided shuttles in the form of open trolley-like cars that were pulled by Allis-Chalmers tractors. There was a driver and a conductor who blew a whistle whenever he wanted to have the tractor driver pick-up or drop off passengers; one blast to stop, two blasts to go ahead. Ten cents a person. The whole tractor/trolley arrangement would weave its way slowly around the fairgrounds and, essentially, allow fairgoers to hitch a ride if they were tired of walking. It was on one of those very trolleys that Mike, when just a very young boy in the early 1950s, had hopped onto when it came past our first stand in front of The Little Theatre. He was mad at mom and dad. They probably had refused him a pony ride or something, and he decided to run away from home, State Fair-style. Paying his dime, he went for a very long ride, a couple of hours, he recalls, and every time the trolley had gone full circuit and went past our stand again, where mom and dad were working, he would duck down and hide. He didn't get very far from "home" and the prodigal son eventually returned only to realize he was never missed.[13]

Friday's were special days for my brothers and me. Back in the 1950s, Fridays were very slow, especially during the day. Consequently, we would have a lot of time to ourselves, sometimes too much time…

"Did you bring it; where is it?"

"Yeah, I've got it" replies Mike to Mark with a nervous smile. Reaching into the right pocket of his blue shorts, Mike, who is eight, pulls out a bright red plastic whistle. Both of them are crouched down just inside and beneath the front counter of our stand

"Are they moving yet?"

"No, he didn't blow the whistle" Mark, six years old, says as he peeks, tippy-toe, over the white-painted wooden countertop. Just a few yards to the left of our stand is an idling big orange tractor with the driver awaiting a signal from the attached passenger trolley. Three fairgoers, an elderly man in a summer hat and two middle-aged women, climb

---

13   That may seem strange or even derelict but, as kids, we felt safe and were considered to be safe anywhere we went in the park - and we did explore every corner

*slowly aboard. They seat themselves along the bench seat that runs the
length of the trolley. On its opposite side, a woman and her two small
kids step off and walk away.*

*"Keep your head down or they'll see us" Mike says, in an unneces-
sarily low voice.*

"OK; are they looking at us?"

"No, it's OK" replies Mark.

*"Tweeeet -- tweeet"... two short blasts of the conductor's high-
pitched whistle fill the boys' ears, shrilly. The driver slowly starts to pull
ahead and begins to pass by Mille's Italian Sausage stand.*

*"Tweeeet" a whistle sounds again, this time slightly higher in tone
and somewhat tentative in its emphasis...sort of what you might expect from a conductor new to the job, and the tractor quickly stops.*

*Peering over the counter top from inside our stand we - all three of
us for I've now joined my brothers - giggle nervously as we see the
pith-helmeted conductor look at the tractor driver while shrugging his
shoulders in the universal gesture of ignorance. With a slight gesture,
the tractor driver is waved on and he, again, moves ahead.*

*"Tweeeet"...and the tractor stops after having moved a mere
twenty feet. The driver, now visibly annoyed, glares back at the assistant who shakes his head to say "no" and, in turn, looks angrily around
the Fair crowd in search of the illegitimate whistle.*

*"What are you boys up to? You didn't put that skunk-oil stuff on
the counter again, did you Mark?" Mom has just walked into the stand
from the entrance at its rear. We look up to her from our huddled position and try to stop giggling.*

*"Nothing, mom, just foolin' around" I say as Mike slides the whistle
back into his pocket, magician-like, and all three of us walk away from
the counter, all angelic.*

...In truth, we were far from angels and had become a real hand-

77

ful for mom, especially with dad working long hours at the restaurant during the other 51 weeks of the year. Much later in life, while paging through an old family photo album, I happened to notice a black and white photograph that had slipped from its mounts. It was a snapshot of Mark, Mike and me from about this period of time and, while trying to re-insert it into the four little corner mounts, I happened to notice handwriting on its back; there, in my mother's unmistakable, perfect penmanship was the penciled notation "The unholy three."

1963

Trout! In the early 1960s, the Fair introduced the pay-to-fish-pond with its swarming mass of brightly colored rainbow trout. This became a frequent destination for both Mark and me. We would study the trout fishing techniques of other anglers as we waited in line – noting, not only whether a fast or slow retrieve worked best but, also, what particular rod, and its associated fly, happened to be hot that day. We would anxiously wait for our group of anglers to be admitted to the fishing area. Nudging our way as close to the front of the line as possible, without irritating too many others, we would wait for the go-ahead. Then, when the man on the microphone gave the OK, we would race off in an attempt to get to the hot fly before someone else grabbed it. This was, however, more than a footrace; it was a matter that involved critical, strategic planning. Was it best to go left and circle around the pond (a big pool actually) which was the shortest route, or to go the longer way to the right since there were fewer competitors moving in that direction? Too, I had to consider the potential speed of each group; maybe it would be better to go with the larger group in the shorter direction to the left – but would I be able to juke-step my way around them to get to the magical rod first? These were tough but important decisions.

Mark and I did very well at the trout pond. The net- handlers began to recognize the two young men in the Mille's T-shirts and would keep their eye on us so they could respond with a quick sweep of the net whenever we hooked-up. One year, Mark spent even more time than usual fishing the trout pond and would bring back two or three trout from every trip...most trips anyway, fishing still being fishing. Later that same summer, soon after the Fair, our family would host the famed Dutch psychic, Peter Hurkos at our home with a dinner of grilled trout. Dad had met him at his restaurant, Michaelangelo's. The trout, of course, all came from the pond at the Wisconsin State Fair.

1965

Just another day here at the Fair...mid-afternoon, there's a pretty good crowd, and I'm strolling the grounds during a cooking break. Walking past the trout pond, I hear the voice of the gray haired manager, which I recognize from my many hours spent there. His voice resonates over the loud speakers:

"Hey Mille – What are ya doin' with the bucket?"

Turning to see why he's calling my name, I realize it's not me he's speaking to. Moving along in his slow, got-all-the-time-in-the-world ambling walk is my grandfather. He's shuffling along, wearing those comfortable old brown shoes, in the line of hopeful anglers moving into position around the perimeter of the tank. With his full head of snow-white hair (partially visible under his gray-blue summer straw Borsalino) and his stocky torso, he could be a southern Italian version of Santa Claus should he decide to grow a beard and add a few pounds. Grandpa has a green plastic bucket in his right hand (it's the one we use to drain ice water at the stand), a folding metal chair in his left, and has stopped dead in his tracks. He turns his head, looking for the source of the inquiring voice that's calling his name...a feigned expression of bewilderment on his tanned, square-jawed face.

"Over here, Mille, by the microphone."

Grandpa's head turns again...right, left, upwards, to the rear...as if to say, "Who's calling me; why is he bothering me?" Then, finally spotting and facing his inquisitor, he replies with a dead-serious expression, "I'mma catcha pesci; needa bigga bucket."

"Who's watching the Italian sausage stand Mille? What are ya doin' goin' fishin'?" the manager asks (as would grandma, were she here).

The banter continues...back and forth...to the amusement of everyone in the area, and I soon realize that these two guys have a regular shtick going on. Nobody in the family, myself included, was aware that grandpa has been doing this routine and, although I know he's capable of most anything that involves fun, I'm still surprised that I've been missing this and just happened to catch it by accident.

"Don't you go using that sausage of yours, no bait fishing here, it's flies only, Mille."

An exaggerated look of disdain, with accompanying hand gestures, is returned and Grandpa now moves into position at the side of the trout tank, turning his back to the would-be game warden. Reaching into the right pocket of his baggy gray slacks, he pulls out a crumpled paper napkin and begins to open its folds. Moments later, its contents are revealed: an Italian sausage, brown and juicy. It obviously was liberated from our grill only recently, as evidenced by the telltale skewer hole in its center. With a quick stab he impales the hefty sausage on the tiny # 12 hook of the delicate trout fly. Taking the rod handle in his right hand, he pokes his arm straight out and pendulums the baited fly out over the water, dooming it to a soggy fate. Grandpa sits down on his now-opened folding chair with an exaggerated look of innocence while his self-tied fly sinks quickly to the bottom and lies there like a chunk of catfish bait.

My grandfather never used anything but a cane pole baited with worms when he fished and that's how he looks right now; the trout rod has become a big ol' cane pole and all he's missing is a bright red and white bobber. To look at him, he could be back on the pier at the old family cottage at Wind Lake catching bluegills and the occasional bullhead. The banter between grandpa and the warden continues as a small oil slick begins to form on the water surface directly above grandpa's line. Anglers on either side gaze into the water, enviously, at his special bait. The trout, however, are unimpressed.

I hang out and watch as the rest of the comedy act unfolds, to the enjoyment of all. Returning to the stand I spill the beans on grandpa's little escapade; it's too special for any of the family to miss and, without letting him know they're onto him, most of them will catch the next matinee. Grandma will take a pass.

Thinking about his routine, later, I realize how fortunate I am - all of us, really - to have such a wonderful grandfather in our lives. No, he may not be a go-getter on the business side, but grandma's got that covered pretty well anyway. He just adds a richness to our own lives with his antics, his stories about his beloved Italy and his big-hearted, good-natured way in general. Life would be much the poorer without him in it.

These were special days. For these few days in August of each year, all of our family was together...grandma and grandpa, working and occasionally bickering, mom frying peppers, all of us kids working a bit and playing a lot, and, of course, there was dad who was running the whole show. It was a time when he was not sharing his time between us and his long hours at the restaurant. We had him for the entire Fair week and he, in turn, was in his glory as he oversaw the success of his many years of effort. On a busy Fair day, when the customers were stacked three-deep and thirty feet across, waving their cash in an attempt to be the next one served, he would have ample proof of what he had accomplished.

Perhaps dad's finest moments were those evenings when the time approached for him to place the order for the next day's supply of sausage and rolls. This was not a trivial exercise nor was it a simple matter. Demand, from day to day, can vary in the extreme and running out of sausage or bread will leave you with nothing to sell on a busy night. Conversely, ordering too much bread could leave you with a lot of expensive, top quality but stale bread that has to be thrown out. Faced with this challenge, dad would be very dramatic at order-placing time, in an obvious, playful sort of way. He would check the weather forecast for the next day, consider the type of entertainment that was lined up for the grandstand, and then pull out his mysterious little notebooks from previous years. Staring at their stained pages, crystal ball-fashion, he read their vital statistics, tea leaves which, if properly interpreted, could offer a glimpse into tomorrow. After assimilating all of the available information, he was ready to ask us kids the big question:

"Mark, how many boxes of sausage are in the walk-in cooler?" then, "Toni - give me a bread count. Give me an honest count, both of you"...as if we had a reason to lie about it. Once we had tallied up the inventory dad would do his math and call in the orders. His forecasts were usually amazingly accurate.

Knowing the importance of the visual aspect of the grill he had invented, dad was always keeping the cooks on their toes by reminding them to have a spit of sausage in front and up high - so passersby would easily notice them. I, when cooking, would find this to be very annoy-

Grandpa in the 1940s

Toni proving she's from
Wisconsin

Mark with a big one from
the State Fair

ing since there's so much to deal with just to do a good job of actually cooking the sausages; the visual part seemed trivial to me, particularly when I was falling behind. I would eventually come-around on this point.

1979

With high expectations, on an early spring morning in 1979 Chuck and I begin our drive to Tucson, by way of Tennessee. All goes well all the way to South Fulton, hard by the Mississippi River, and only after picking up the new concession trailer do we run into problems. Somewhere in central Texas while driving through a sleet storm we realize we've lost power to the refrigeration unit and the weather only serves to emphasize our sudden reversal of fortune. With hundreds of pounds of fresh Italian sausage at risk, finding a diesel refrigeration unit repairman at 11:00 p.m. on Interstate I-20 seems an impossibility but, somehow, we find a guy who is able to come out to help us. A few hours later, with our spirits refreshed, we head west again.

Tucson is a breath of fresh air. We are in the real Arizona now – not the Arizona of Phoenix to the north with its transposed easterners who bring their well-watered green lawns with them. No, Tucson in 1979 is real desert with real westerners, or at least the parts that I'm seeing are. After getting set up, I interview and hire a handful of teenagers to work the counters. All of them are local kids whose families have lived in

Arizona for generations. These kids talk about finding
Indian pots in the desert and about their horses. One
of them, a tiny girl, tells me her parents just gave her a
new bull rope for her sixteenth birthday, and she's very
excited about it. A bull rope is something that's used
in rodeos. The would-be rider of a half-wild Brahma
bull secures him or her self to the bull by wrapping the
rope around the bull and their hand just before someone does something very offensive to the bull. He then
opens the chute to allow him - the bull - to express
his dissatisfaction. This is a petite girl of sixteen. I feel
like I'm on another planet but I thoroughly enjoy the
experience of meeting and working with people with
such a different life-experience. Back home, most of
the teenaged girls I know expect something a bit more
trendy and fashionable than a rope for their sixteenth
birthdays. Expensive clothes, electronics, gala parties
versus...a bull rope - and I think the Tucson version
of sweet-sixteen was more thrilled than her eastern
counterparts.

The Italian sausage sales go well and the Tucson
people are, predictably, intrigued by the unique charcoal grill. Many fairgoers experience their first Italian
sausage sandwich and, after a good run, we shut down
and point the truck and trailer east where we will re-
supply and prepare for our next engagement. It's been
a good start.

WE ACCEPT HER,
ONE OF US

SATURDAY 6:20 P.M.

"ALWAYS COUNT THE CUSTOMER'S CHANGE BACK TO THEM TO AVOID or catch any mistakes...and then thank them for their order..." I'm still training the young kids in the small stand on how to take and fill orders. Since we serve beer at the big stand, the kids there have to be at least 18 years of age. We get most of the younger teens here at the small stand. For many of them this is their first job outside of their home and it's usually obvious. But they catch-on very quickly and, although I constantly have to remind them to not overfill (and spill) the Cokes, they have a lot of energy and almost always work out pretty well.

A couple of the girls have started to respond to the smiles of the french fries boys next door; within a day or so I'll have to start chasing the boys away so our customers can get to our counter. It happens at about this time every Fair.

Over the years we've had hundreds of boys and girls work at Mille's and some of the old timers will stop by to say hi; sometimes with their own kids in tow, who usually are surprised to learn that this was where their mom or dad had their first job. The cooks…now they're a different breed. They've always been guys, but only because a woman hasn't stepped forward yet. They've been young, old, short, tall, experienced and inexperienced. Businessmen, tradesmen, students, an opera singer, a state trooper and at least one hippy (in the 70's of course) all worked as cooks here at Mille's. A few years ago, those many fairgoers who are also ardent golfers would have been startled to know that the young man flipping spits on the grill in front of them, Steve Anderson - Mark's brother-in-law, Donna's brother - had been on the Nike professional golf tour before working at our stand. Playing at Escondido Country Club in California, he once tied a course record of 64 that he shares with top tour pro Mark Wiebe. The record, as far as I know, still stands; not bad for a sausage cook. Yes, they've come in all sizes, shapes, and forms…heck, we even had a one-legged cook. He, on a hot day, would sometimes remove his prosthetic and jump around on his one leg while tending to the grill - quite a sight. He worked hard and did a good job, but he eventually quit. Anyway, in retrospect, it's probably not a good idea having people with obviously missing appendages working in a sausage operation - it raises too many questions and causes customers to look too closely (unnecessarily) at the sausage in their sandwich; it's just bad for business.

It's difficult to anticipate how a new cook is going to work out. Some take right to it while others throw up their arms in frustration and quit before they even get a full day in. It's a tough job.

1959

Just five days ago grandpa had the stand dragged down the street by the cowboy and it's still holding up all right. People are gathering in front of the charcoal grill more than usual; a man points to the grill and is saying something to the others. I can't hear him but his smile and the smiles of his friends suggest they like what they see. Not unusual, that, but there's something about his focus – that pointing finger that grabs my own attention – so I walk towards grandpa who is tending the grill (which, in itself, is unusual). Leaning over the counter to see the front of the grill, I now understand what has stopped them in their tracks; Amatore, Senior – grandpa – has a spit of skewered lamb chops hanging on the front of the grill and, if it's possible for anything to look more succulent than roasting sausages, it could only be lamb chops.

These are not those thick, short-boned fancy chops they serve at expensive restaurants; these are the thinner, long boned chops that may not be as fancy but taste the best of all. Grandpa smiles and gives me the old, corner-of-the-mouth-twist-with-the-fingers gesture, as in "wait till-a you tasta dis…mangiare!" But he doesn't say that, doesn't have to; the gesture wasn't even necessary (although, being Italian, irrepressible), the long-handled chops, marbled and well-browned, speak for themselves. He then lifts the spit and rests the tip on the edge of the ash pit and, with his other hand, takes a handful of grated Romano cheese from a small bowl and sprinkles it all along that full spit of chops, first one side, then the other. Putting the spit back on the grill he instructs me "Amatore- watcha-clos', non burn-a formagg'." A minute later, he lifts the entire spit and, as he walks to the kitchen with it, the eyes of the people in front of the stand follow him like he has taken their gourmet dinner plate away after having just removed the silver lid. They can't follow him into the kitchen area but I can and do. Grandpa

89

takes the long two-pronged fork and uses it to slide the lamb chops off the spit. Within moments my mouth is filled with the taste of succulent lamb, those long bones being the only eating utensils needed. This is the way to eat a lamb chop - how else could you gnaw right down to the bone and get every bit of this delicious meat? When I'm finally done, I throw the bone (which now looks like something that's been lying in the sand, bleached by the desert sun) into the garbage pail and grab another chop. Through the kitchen screen partition, I see and hear the pointy-fingered customer asking the young Mille's T-shirted waitress about the lamb chops. With a teen-ager's first-job awkwardness, she is smiling nervously, pointing to grandpa, who's also on his second chop; she's telling the man that we don't sell them, that "the grandpa" just grilled them for dinner. The man looks very disappointed. Grandma has now joined us and she tells me..."mangiare", *always concerned that her grandson was too skinny. I wasn't, and I really didn't need any encouragement but that's just how it is with an Italian grand-mother. As I finish off my second chop and consider another, I notice that grandpa's wearing his same old brown leather belt today, the one with the six unused belt holes. The holes are on the fat side of the buckle and, since I can't recall him ever being heavier, I wonder if he's just planning ahead.*

Later, mom is at the cash register and my buddy Richie, who's been hanging out in the park all day (he sneaks into the park by climbing over the fence near the old harness racing stables) asks me if I can take a break with him to go see Stutze the Pinhead Girl...again. Mom laughs..."You two boys and that pinhead girl; what's the big deal?"

"You should see her, mom, she's got this pointy little head and she just sits there, over in the freak show tent."

"All right, go ahead" *she smiles and hands me two singles knowing I'll pay Richie's way in too...and he would never hesitate to accept her favors.*

90

Richie was a great con man, especially for a fifteen-year old kid. Eddie Haskell had nothing on Richie; my mother liked him, or maybe she just felt sorry for him, knowing he had problems at home. He pulled off some amazing things - many of which were actually very funny. A few days before the Fair started, I had convinced him to go fishing with me at an old stone quarry way out on Greenfield Avenue. We took my brothers Mike and Mark along since they liked to fish too. Mom agreed to drive the four of us out there and, after stopping at Bob's Bait on highway 100 for some big, juicy night crawlers, she dropped us off at the quarry. She looked worried (she often did) but we assured her we'd be O.K. We spent the afternoon exploring the rocky banks of the quarry and did some serious fishing as well but, by the end of the day, we had caught only one fish. It was some strange kind of silvery baitfish, only about 5 inches long. Not even I, after having spent most of my youth reading and re-reading stacks of fishing magazines which towered precariously next to my twin bed, was able to identify it. Deciding to finally hang it up, we left the banks of the old quarry lake and stood at the side of Greenfield Avenue. There, we began to hitchhike. Hitching a ride was something we did a lot of back then, but, on this day, we were not able to get anyone to stop and pick us up, not even with me on my crutches and my leg in a cast. Finally, hot and tired, Richie took over. He had my brothers and me hide in the brush away from the road. Taking my crutches, he stood on the side of the road in front of a telephone pole. Bending his right leg behind him and using the telephone pole to hold it up and out of sight, he stuck out his thumb. With my crutches under his armpits, supporting him, this poor, rail-thin, one-legged boy adopted a forlorn expression that not even his flashy Hollywood hairstyle (long and slicked back on the sides, flat-top crew cut on top) could betray. When Richie put on his "lost-puppy-about-to-be-put-to-sleep" face, he was not to be denied. Within moments, my brothers and I heard the screeching of brakes and watched as a blue and white Chevy Bel Air came to a sudden stop. Taking just a few crutch-assisted steps to the car, Richie opened the rear door, dropped the crutches to the ground and hopped in...looking for all-the-world like some miraculously healed repentant. Mike, Mark, and I quickly, or as quickly as I could manage with a bum leg, left our hiding spot and got into the car next to my buddy, picking up my crutches on the way. The driver of the car, a man in his forties with too-thick eyebrows that begged to be trimmed, looked at us and seemed lost for words; so Richie, never afraid to speak, spoke instead... "Can you drop us off at 82nd and Greenfield? Thanks!"

Now, at the fairgrounds with the two dollars from my mother in my pocket, Richie and I are making our way over the short distance to Grandstand Avenue where we turn right. There we come to the canvas-sided freak show tent with it's huge, garish, carnival-art style paintings that promise a once-in-a-lifetime sight, although Richie and I have seen it four times already just at this Fair. We listen to the barker's loud pleadings to "Step right up, don't be shy, step right up." We've heard the rest of his pitch quite a few times so I just step to the ticket seller's counter and buy two tickets. We're then prompted into the dimly lit, foreboding, tent. It's a relatively small area and there are already a half dozen or so other voyeurs standing around. After about five minutes, a normal but very bored appearing older woman walks through a slit in the canvas tent wall. Holding her hand is who we've all come to see - Stutze. Wearing a loose fitting dress, the diminutive Stutze is unlike anyone who these fairgoers, excepting Richie and me, have ever seen. Her head, shaved, save a little topknot to emphasize its shape, truly comes to a well-defined point and she looks half human, half something else. Stutze and her assistant just sit in a large chair for a few minutes, quite unmindful of the gawkers who, after a few quiet *minutes, gradually slip out of the tent speaking to each other in hushed tones as they depart. An air of awkward embarrassment is present as they, and eventually Richie and I, leave the tent. We have no idea why we keep coming back to this macabre scene but we do and I will remember that freak show forever.*

SATURDAY 6:45 P.M.

The Sky Glider moves along its cable, high above the fairgrounds. Its passengers overlook a panorama of thousands of fairgoers in a slow moving migration to no place in particular. Down below, there is a couple sunning themselves on the roof of El Vagabond, the Mexican food stand across from us on Second Street. The guy with the sunglasses holds a drink on high, toasting the passengers as they pass overhead. He does it all day long, all week long. Eleven days all told. It's been going on for several years now. The scantily clad couple are mannequins that the El Vagabond folks pose on their roof, just for yuks. We all know that, of course. They haven't moved an inch since the Fair started; same deal last year, and we look right out to that scene from the big stand.

"Doesn't that guy ever move up there?" asks a puzzled Roy to no one in particular as he gazes out from his usual position at the side of the grill. Mike looks at me with a squinched-up brow and slight smile. He's obviously thinking something like "you gotta be kidding!" but he doesn't say anything.

"Roy, why don't you go up there and ask if they want a beer?" Mike is smiling and Roy realizes something's funny and he's at the center of it.

"What?" Roy asks with a smile, already joining in on the monotony-breaking humor knowing he's the target. The thing about

Roy is, he can laugh at anything and anyone, including himself, and just doesn't mind if we pick on him a bit. He knows that we only tease the ones we love and that he can give it back to us anytime he wants; he frequently does and, with his quick wit, doesn't pull any punches. The thing is, though, when things are getting dicey and we need someone to step in and get some sausage grilled in a hurry or help out with any of a number of daily emergencies - we can count on Roy. Same deal with Brian and all of the regulars that work with us each year. It would be a very long day without them. And in the case of Roy, lest anyone start to feel sorry for the poor, beleaguered fellow, know that every year, without fail, this charcoal-dusted bachelor is the one that all of the pretty waitresses flock to. Go figure.

Roy enjoys the humor of the situation once we clue him in. For years, Roy has worked as a cook at Mike and Mary's restaurant, Mille's Spaghetti Factory, in Mequon, a suburb of Milwaukee. This will soon end when they retire from the restaurant business and begin to have weekends to themselves again, something they've not had for about thirty years. They will, of course, continue on with Toni, Mark, and me in the State Fair operation as well as in their other summer gig at Summerfest, a large annual festival held at Milwaukee's lakefront.

Mike has, for years now, filled the shoes of dad as the restaurateur in the family. We should have seen it coming. Even as a little kid, Mike had been given responsibilities far beyond the norm for someone his age. When only eight he would sometimes be given the morning's cash bank in a brown paper bag to take out to the park. I'm talking about a little kid...what, second grade, maybe? ... carrying a couple of hundred dollars in bills and rolled coins while walking from our home all the way to the fairgrounds.

That seems risky looking back on it - but, then again, who would have suspected? Maybe it's a testimony to the times as well. And then there was that day...in the 1960s. We were teenagers and the Klement's Sausage delivery guy was unloading the morning's sausage supply. He was a round and pink-faced, heavy man who looked like he had worked with pork and sausages for a very long time...had even begun to take on their physical characteristics, much like a dog owner will resemble his pet much more often than mere coincidence can account for. As always, his white hardhat was perched precariously on his too-big of a head. How dangerous, we wondered, could a falling sausage really be? On that particular day, he had his kid along while he made his deliveries. As we were doing our morning routines, we heard the little boy, maybe seven or eight years old and a good-eater himself, say to his dad in a kid's too-loud of a whisper,

"*Dad – see him?*"... pointing with his chin towards our brother Mike who was, prophetically, preparing the cash register for the day..."*That's Mike - he's gonna own this whole stand someday*" his reverent tone implying that they were looking at the heir to something that rivaled the Uihlein family's Schlitz Brewery fortune. Toni, Mark, and I looked suspiciously at Mike, then at the kid, and then went on with our work.

Now, all these years later, Mike will teasingly remind the three of us what the safety-conscious deliveryman's little boy predicted. But, in a way, it is true. Mike did step into the family restaurant business, but in a cruel irony, being the only sibling working full time in the restaurant business, here at the State Fair he, along with Mary, has additional, difficult responsibilities that the rest of us do not. The most stressful is, perhaps, the pressure of the daily sausage and bread order. With the tradition of dad's uncanny forecasting ability hanging over him like the Sword of Damocles, Mike asks us to give him an honest count of the remaining inventory towards the end of each day. We tease him about it but, without having to say a word, we all know that the pressure to get it right is tremendous and a significant miscalculation will hit us all in our pocketbooks. So we give him an honest count and he gives us his honest efforts and we all appreciate it but never really tell him.

1983

Mark is still a bachelor as Fair week arrives. We've all, at least most of us, given up on him ever marrying and that's all right. He is a very solitary individual and, as an artist, seems to prefer peace and quiet. As a married man, with children, I also value peace and quiet but just don't get much of it.

The latest in a series of pleasant young women from a Milwaukee family is working for us again this year. Donna, a very nice, intelligent and attractive blond, is following in the footsteps of her sisters, Chris and Julie. Donna drives but her sisters before her would get dropped off and picked up at the fairgrounds by their mother every day. It was a hassle for her but she put up with it as long as the girls continued to bring home a couple of sausage sandwiches every night. Donna now shares each day's experiences with her mother, including the goings-on at the big stand where she works. She tells her about Mike, married to Mary, who is outgoing and very personable; all the good ones are already taken. Mark, the single brother, is, on the other hand, good looking but not very friendly; he gives her orders and doesn't smile a whole lot. He's also a bit of a mystery - an artist, she believes. This seems to be confirmed when she notices the softness of his hands when she takes change from him at the cash register.

Toni has not given up on finding a mate for her brother, never mind the fact that he's not even looking. As this year's Fair is drawing to a close she has suggested we have a drink or two at a local pub after shutting down. This is unusual for us as we are usually so tired by the end of the Fair that we just want to go home and collapse; I suspect she has something up her sleeve. Her ulterior motive becomes clear when I hear her invite Donna to join us for drinks. The plot thickens. Donna accepts the invite and shows up at a pub in the nearby village of Wauwatosa. In this relaxed social setting, Mark starts to open up and we all notice that he and Donna spend quite a bit of time together in conversation. Hmmmm.

Five weeks later, the telephone rings in a Milwaukee home. It is answered by Donna's sister Chris.

"Hello"

"Hi, this is Mark, from Mille's."

"Oh, hi Mark, how are you?"

"Real good...is Donna home...may I talk to her?"

"Yeah, sure...where do you want her to work?"

"Nowhere...I want to ask her out."

1985

I'm together with good friends and I've just slipped the rental video into the VCR. We're all in a great mood and share a heightened anticipation as I push the play button on the remote; they've all been prepped for what we're about to see. Earlier this week, while browsing through the old classics section of TLA Video in Philadelphia, I happened to notice a movie titled FREAKS subtitled, THE STORY OF THE LOVE LIFE OF THE SIDESHOW. Looking back at me, from the cover of the illustrated video box was, after all these 26 years...Stutze the Pinhead Girl herself. Unaware that this film from 1932 had actually reached cult status in recent years (hence its appearance at my video store) I felt that I had stumbled upon a part of my youth and quickly looked over the rest of the box's teasers...

"Do Siamese twins make love?"

"Can a full grown woman truly love a midget?"

"What sex is the half man half woman?"

And, finally, "Louella Parsons says - For pure sensationalism FREAKS *tops any picture yet produced. It's more fantastic and grotesque than any shocker ever written."*

Having heard me talk about Stutze in the past, my friends were eager to see what the big deal was all about (just like mom back in 1959). The movie starts and, after a while, Stutze is on the screen and I, too enthusiastically, shout out -

"It's Stutze, right there, Stutze..."

We then settle in to watch this very weird movie. The advertising on the video box is, if anything, understated. The movie evolves around the lives of sideshow freaks, played by actual "freaks" like Stutze[14], and the wedding of one of them, the midget Hans, to a normal woman, the beautiful trapeze artist, Cleopatra. In what is the most haunting scene of the entire movie, all of the freaks, including Stutze, are sitting around the wedding table chanting:

"Gooble-gobble, gooble-gobble, we accept her, we accept her, one of us, one of us."

---

14 The movie credits indicate that the pinhead girl is "Schlitze" but I know better. It is Stutze, plain as day. In doing the research for this book, I came to realize that the pinhead girl "Schlitze" actually appeared under various names when she toured, which explains the discrepancy. More surprisingly, I learned that Stutze/Schlitze was actually a man but for promotional purposes he was always billed as the "pinhead girl".

And so the beautiful woman is welcomed into the unique carnival family.

1979

I've been thinking about Sisyphus recently. He's the poor sap from Greek mythology who pissed-off the gods in some very significant way and was punished by having to push a huge boulder up a steep incline, only to have it roll back down each time it reaches the summit. As if this weren't bad enough, the real tragedy of Sisyphus is that he knows that the boulder will always roll back down the hill. There is no hope for Sisyphus – his task is eternal.

After the Tucson spring debut, I returned, temporarily, to my day job here in Michigan selling information technology products and services to large companies. I know that, if I remain in this job, I will work hard to achieve my sales quota and, regardless of how well I perform, will have to start all over again come January 1st. I am not accumulating any form of equity and I will be starting at zero all over again – and again, and again; Sisyphus and me. But, over the next few months, I intend to complete my plans, resign from this job, and hit the summer circuit with the mobile sausage wagon. I will begin to build something for myself and my family and I will do it in the enjoyable environment of fairs – just like back in Wisconsin every August.

Then, in June,1979, I finally resign from my job

with my employer of twelve years. Within days my road partner Chuck and I are headed for Winnipeg, Manitoba where we will operate at a very large fair known as the Red River Exhibition. I am replete with the excitement of finally launching my new venture and my optimism knows no limits. After a drive of a couple of days, we arrive at Red River Exhibition Park, locate our designated spot and get set-up. A number of the fair circuit regulars seem to be quite intrigued by our unique charcoal grill and they introduce themselves to Chuck and me. Although my family has operated in Wisconsin for so many years, I've never really inter-acted with the carnie-types before, so this is a first for me. What a different world it is! Very decent people but many of them view their business very differently from the Mille approach. I get my first sense of that when I'm talking with a guy who runs the corn-dog concession next to our spot. He and I are standing behind my trailer (or, "joint" as he refers to it) and he's noticed that I've just had to tell one of the teen-aged girls that I've hired to clean up her mess in the kitchen area.

"Did you hire an extra?"

"What do you mean?" I ask.

"You should always hire an extra kid; one more than you really need."

"Why's that?"

"With these kids, you've got to get their attention right away. I always hire one more kid than I need and the first time I see one of them screwing around, I fire the kid right on the spot. Scares the shit outta the others and you won't have any problems the rest of the fair…but you have to do it in front of the whole crew so they all see it." He chuckles in a voice that seems tired and hard. Later that week, we talk about profit margins and ratio of labor costs to sales revenues; he clearly has a firm grip on his business interests but he never speaks of the quality of his corn-dogs or of family.

On my breaks, I like to walk around the Exposition grounds and see what's going on…see what different types of food products and other attractions are present. As is typical, the midway with its loud music and bright, sequentially- flashing chaser lights is the most popular attraction and I enjoy just strolling around and taking in the sights and sounds. While there, I eventually have a vague sense of something missing or not quite right but cannot put my finger on it. The ethereal feeling remains unidentified, and I return to the wagon and my work. We eventually complete our run in Winnipeg but the odd sensation stays just out of touch, like some misty dream vestige seeking my attention, refusing to depart unnoticed.

Just as with Tucson, for our first year, this fair has been very promising and suggests significant future success. I have stayed with the staff that I originally hired and did have to keep after them from time to time…but never had to fire anyone. Our next stop on our Canadian circuit is to one of the greatest fairs in the world, The Calgary Stampede, and I look forward to being in the real west again.

1986

As our individual lives have progressed and evolved it has become difficult for the entire family to come together other than at the Fair. Toni and I both live on the east coast now and, other than at State Fair time, we usually are not all re-united during any particular year, not even at Christmas, not all of us anyway. The constraints imposed by limited vacation allowances and other demands combine in a tyranny of time - there's just not enough of it available.

But today is different. We are all together again and we're not at the Fair; nor has anyone died. It's the evening of November 1st, 1986 and I'm sitting next to and talking with my eleven- year old niece, Melissa - "Missy" to all of us. I am watching for my opportunity. Since she was a very young girl I have been able to sucker her into falling for the old nose-flick trick, the one where I get her to look down at an imaginary stain on her blouse, or, for variety, at the necklace she's wearing which I'm pointing to - then, of course, having been caught off-guard, she receives a quick flick of the thumb to the down-turned nose. I used to get her all the time but now she's older and wiser and each year it becomes more difficult to trick her. I'm sure she has prepared for this day by telling herself, repeatedly, "I'm not going to fall for it, I'm not going to fall for it…" Before I make my attempt, however, I am inter-rupted by the high-pitched "clink–clink-clink" of a crystal champagne flute being tapped repeatedly by a knife - or perhaps a spoon or fork. Within seconds, other "clinks" in varying pitch and tone have joined in, creating a cacophony of banquet room noise. I and every one else, save the scurrying wait-staff, stop all activity and conversation and, slowly, the large elegant room becomes very quiet. Mark, striking in his black tux, rises from his seat at the head table, here in the Nantucket Shores restaurant in downtown Milwaukee. Seated next to him on his left is a young woman who he first met when she applied for a waitress job at Mille's Italian Sausage at the Wisconsin State Fair. Donna has just become the newest member of the Mille family. Mark goes on to state some very heart-felt sentiments on this most-sentimental of days and I am moved by his ability to express his private emotions as well as he does. Clearly, Donna has gotten through to the very quiet, private young man and she, in turn, has experienced the old adage of still but deep waters.

Donna is beautiful in her wedding dress and they obviously are both very happy. I am struck by the notion of how interesting it is that our annual eleven day family gathering - the cooking and selling of Italian sausage sandwiches - is such a strong anchor point for our entire family that it not only brings us together year after year, generation after generation, but has now reached a new significance by actually contributing to the very growth of our family.

Mark finishes his loving remarks and we all raise our champagne flutes in a toast to the new married couple. As we cheer the momentous event I also can't help but welcome Donna in my own way to our special carnival family as I silently recall - "We accept her, we accept her, one of us, one of us."

1965

A lovely, young lyric soprano in a beautiful lilac velvet dinner suit steps to the center of the stage. She looks up to five magnificent levels of hanging balconies that climb forever and surround the expanse of main floor seating in a dramatic, flaring horseshoe-shaped arc. Elite boxes, specially designed and occupied in an earlier era by patrons named Astor and Vanderbilt, outline the form of this Diamond Horseshoe, as it is called. A towering, painted, domed ceiling, reminiscent of the

103

Sistine Chapel and rich with sculpted, classical figures dominates all. It is the late afternoon of Thursday March 25th, 1965 and the setting is the stage of the Metropolitan Opera House in New York. The young lady is my sister Toni, "Antoinette Mille" on the afternoon's program. Our mother, Alice, proudly looks on from the floor of the main level as Antoinette steps to the beautiful grand piano.

Toni's journey here, to the Met, was preceded by many years of study and practice but only in recent years as a singer. Never losing her passion for the performing arts that was first kindled in The Little Theatre at the Wisconsin State Fair, she studied to be a classical pianist but it was during a summer family vacation at a Wisconsin dude ranch while still a young girl that she was urged to study voice. She did and, a few, short years later, after achieving significant success in Milwaukee and Chicago competitions, was advised to enter the Metropolitan Opera Company's national talent search. In this program, hundreds of singers from all across the U.S, Canada, and Australia would be competing with the regional winners going to New York to perform at the Met itself, the old, original Metropolitan Opera House.[15] She entered the auditions and, with only five years of vocal training, Antoinette just kept on winning right through the Midwest regional competition which was held in Minneapolis.

Now, here at the Met, she steps into the bend of the grand piano and waits for the opening notes from the pianist. Unknown to her, she is being watched closely by a very important and famous woman whose presence and attention will be vitally significant in her career. As she looks out over the awe-inspiring setting in front of her, she thinks of, and feels the presence of, Enrico Caruso who had once stood on this

---

15 This revered old landmark, which would be replaced just one year later by the new Met at Lincoln Center, had been the site of the greatest operatic performances in America since it first opened in 1883.

very stage, on this very spot. Her thoughts go to grandpa, that lover of all things Italian; he will be impressed and proud when she tells him. It was he who introduced her, as a little girl, to opera and the great Caruso. How she, a very young child, had looked forward to their Sunday morning radio "dates" together when grandpa would carefully tune the family Victrola to the opera program – for just the two of them. The anticipation of the singing they would hear on Sundays would make those times together very special. Grandma will be impressed too; she's not here but she has used her master seamstress skills to make the velvet dinner dress Antoinette wears and which rivals the couture of the most exclusive New York fashion shops.

Mom, watching from the main floor with other members of the live audience, momentarily flashes back in her mind's eye and sees her excited little girl running from the back of the Italian sausage stand and across the grass to the Little Theatre so many years ago. But she is pulled back into the moment as Antoinette begins to sing DORETTA'S SONG. Starting slowly, her pure-toned voice starts low and gradually rises to the demanding high notes while sublimely embracing the lyrics with her own sensitive and emotionally-rich interpretation. The beautifully placed voice easily sustains the intense phrases, all the while embracing the emotions of the moment. Mom feels a warm, tingling sensation on the back of her neck while her eyes begin to mist. Her daughter has come a long way from her first inspiration within The Little Theatre of The Wisconsin State Fair - a very long way indeed! A few minutes later Antoinette ends the aria to a very loud, appreciative applause. She has absolutely nailed it and the judges all realize this. She has become the first Wisconsinite to reach the finals at the Met.

It is now four days later, Monday March 29th and Toni and mom are back in Milwaukee. A Western Union messenger comes to the door and presents a telegram, addressed to my sister. She opens the yellow envelope and begins to read...

*"Miss Antoinette Mille, Congratulations on wonderful perfor-
mance. Prepared to offer you to tour with Metropolitan Opera National Company. Please respond immediately." Suddenly, seeing the
signature at the bottom of the yellow telegram, she becomes aware that
she has been noticed by one of her lifelong idols.
"Sincerely, Rise Stevens" she finishes. Both she and mom are
speechless. Miss Stevens, one of America's greatest mezzo-sopranos,
had dominated the Met's stage for over twenty years and is now the
director of the Met's new National Touring Company. She, personally,
is offering Toni an opportunity of a lifetime. My big sister is about to
represent the Metropolitan Opera Company and do so at the international level. For her, the State Fair with its seminal influence and the
annual family business reunion will be put on hold while she performs
in every major city in the US and clear across Canada with the year's
tour ending in Mexico City and Guadalajara. Six years earlier, a de-
molition crew had swung their huge, rusted iron wrecking balls into
the walls of the Little Theatre leaving nothing but dust and rubble but,
for my sister, the stage is alive and well.*

1969

*The weather forecast is threatening. We're used to dealing with
big storms, summer thunderstorms during the dog days of August,
and we sometimes deal with rains of biblical proportion that turn the
fairgrounds into an instant water park. The younger fairgoers enjoy
the slipping and sliding while stomping through the deepest puddles
they can find. But this weather, today, is different. Toni ("Antoinette"
seems way too formal for the State Fair) is back with the family again
and she has brought along some help. It was while touring with the*

*Metropolitan Opera Company that she met and fell in love with an-
other vocalist, Walter Adkins. They became engaged and she has now
returned to Wisconsin with her fiancée, his two young children Carl
and Mary, and many stories of far-away opera houses and glamorous
people. The family feels doubly-blessed; not only do we have my sister
back but, with Walter, we have a soon-to-be new family member and,
while we admire his operatic ability, more importantly...he already
shows promise on the grill.*

*It is the last year of our temporary, knockdown stand here at the
Fair. Grandma, in her sleeveless house dress with the mustard colored
flowers and an equally colorful floral-patterned apron tied around her
ample waist (flowers on top of flowers...never too many flowers) is slicing bread in the partitioned-off kitchen area while, across the dividing
barrier, mom is at the register, Mike is pouring beers, Toni is waiting
on customers, Walter mans the grill and his kids pour Cokes every now
and then. Grandma has just been telling twelve year old Carl to haul
some boxes of bread back into the kitchen for her but grandpa, from
where he stands on the customer side of the counter, tells her to leave the
young boy alone, he's working too hard; this opinion, of course, is based
on grandpa's standards, not grandma's. He secretly flashes a wink and
a sly smile to Carl and leisurely strolls away.*

*Severe storm warnings have been issued and the earlier jaundice
sky has shifted from cautionary yellow to near full-dark, with swirly
clouds scudding all about. Mom is worried and frightened. She has
always feared summer thunderstorms, something that I don't understand. For me the thunder and lightning is something to be in awe of,
the unbridled force of nature at its most powerful and invigorating.
For her, severe storms required the frantic herding of us kids down
to the basement. There, she would try to lead us in the saying of the
rosary while I would go upstairs every few minutes under the guise of*

checking on the storm. In truth, I reveled in the displays of wind and lightening but did poorly with the rosary.[16]

Mom's fear has now become extreme, even for her, but in this instance she has cause...for we are about to be hit by a storm unlike anything we've ever seen. While a couple of male customers stand at the front counter of the canvas roofed stand, two Schlitz delivery guys haul cases of empties out of the stand and cart full cases back in. Then, it hits. Full cups of beer and one of Coke fly off our counter and sparks explode from the grill as a tremendous wind hits the stand. Shrieks of fairgoers are soon drowned-out by a roaring sound that has no visible source nor any discernible direction...it is just everywhere...a freight train with no tracks and no direction. It all happens so fast...the men at the counter jump into the stand for some degree of protection...a straw to a drowning man for we are no safer here...and the Schlitz men act quickly, herding Carl and Mary onto the sawdust covered ground of the floorless stand, they then have the women huddle over the children. But grandma is on the other side of the mandatory divider that separates beer service from kitchen area so Toni and Walter rush to help her. Within moments she understands that she has to get herself under the three-foot high barrier and tries to bend down, but she is now 77 years old and not nimble. In one of those spontaneous moments of crises when emotions run rampant and contradictory, grandma begins to laugh at herself and the situation she is in, trying to bend beneath the barrier,

---

16 Only many years later did she explain the basis of her phobia to her granddaughter, Therese. During her depression-era childhood, she had shared an attic bedroom with her sisters. The cramped, largely unfinished space was insulated with straw, a cheap material that even her family could afford. One evening during a thunderstorm the house was struck by lightening and an attic fire ensued, fueled by the straw. Fortunately, no one died in the fire nor was anyone seriously injured, but the incident does explain her fear and urge to get as far below the roof of her home as possible.

Carl waking grandpa from
his nap

Antoinette at The Met.
She's come a long way
from The Little Theatre!

Donna and Mark; we accept
her, one of us

modestly pressing the front of her dress to her bosom, and Toni begins to laugh as well. Finally, she makes it through and fear becomes dominant again. With the women all accounted for, the Schlitz men and the other guys form a protective canopy over the women and children as the roar heightens...and, with debris flying all about, the cyclone-like winds increase and eventually subside. From inside the huddled mass a woman's voice - mom's - asks, "where's your grandfather?" As the pile melts, eyes look at each other, asking the question without speaking it... "where's grandpa?" Nobody knows. Sirens are now screaming as rescue vehicles rush to areas where they are needed. Directly across Second Street, the scaffold that is used for the performances of The Kids From Wisconsin has collapsed and it is not certain if anyone has been injured. But what about grandpa? Who saw him last? Nobody seems to know and worry increases as answers fall short. The stand itself, being wide-open all around, survived the winds, which just blew straight through with nothing offering much resistance. As cups and napkins, chairs, bread boxes, and assorted other bric-a-brac are swept up and picked-up, concern mounts for our missing grandfather. Time passes, customers return, and all is back to business as usual but grandpa still has not shown up and now everyone is very concerned. Surely, if he were hurt someone would have helped him and we would have been notified...the cops all know him, so there should be nothing to worry about. Right? Now, it's been an hour and Mike decides its time to walk over to the Police Building and ask about him, so my 21 year old brother leaves the stand, walking out the back entry way. As he exits the stand, he suddenly stops...there, directly in front of him is his grandfather, unconscious. Not the victim of the storm, however, but simply fast asleep in the passenger seat of the family car, oblivious to the weather and the concerns of everyone.

As the crowd slowly and gradually departs the park late on this Saturday all of us are eager to shut down, make the drive home (my sister, Tyler, and I are bunking-up at Mike and Mary's house) and get into the shower to remove the dust and smoke. Then we'll get about six hours of sleep before starting all over again. We've seen a few tipsy fairgoers tonight, although not as many as usual for a Saturday, and they've not been particularly obnoxious. It's been a good night. "Hey - which one of you girls is Mille?" the 20-something guy who has just walked across the mall from the Budweiser pavilion asks. The teen-aged girls at the counter don't know what to say and look around at Toni and me with uncomfortable smiles that ask for help. We are very protective of the young kids who work for us and are always watching-out for them, particularly late on a Friday or Saturday night.

"It's not a woman's name; you're thinking of the name m-i-l-l-i-e" (I spell it out) "our family name is "m-i-l-l-e, no i - she's a Mille (nodding towards my sister), I'm a Mille" all the time thinking to myself, why do I bother? But I go on "...Mille is Italian for thousand as in a Mille lire note, or the Mille Miglia sports car race." This guy really doesn't care and I tell the two girls to go in the back and get some more cups for the Coke fountains; we don't really need them but I want to get them away from this drunk, both to protect them and to remove the attraction.

"Would you like a sandwich?"

"How much are them brats?"

"Four dollars" (I decide to not start a dialogue on the differences between bratwurst and Italian sausage).

111

"Nah, got any beer?"

"No, just Coke and Sprite." He stumbles away, and the girls come back out.

It's now about thirty minutes later and we've finally closed up and walked back to the big stand; they've had a little later push than us because they do serve beer and are just in the final steps of closing up. The coals have been knocked down and the ashes and grease are being hauled out by Roy and Joe. Joe is a young man, currently a college student, who lives across the street from our old family home not far from the State Fair. He and his sister Becky have been regulars with us for a number of years and do a great job working primarily in the kitchen of the big stand, wrapping sandwiches and spitting sausage. Joe also likes to talk about sports and we often debate the fortunes of the Packers versus the Eagles or the Brewers versus the Phillies; helps us get through a very long day.

Brian, after a day of hard work and ample State Fair delicacies, removes his still nearly spotless green apron and hangs the long garment on a specific nail protruding from the kitchen framework...no fancy closets at Mille's. He will try to get several days of wear out of this apron. This is an act of cost-consciousness which ought to be recognized and rewarded as well as a competitive thing between him and Roy. Although equally skilled in his cooking, Roy is not known for his neatness and his green apron in never green for long. Brian leaves the kitchen, done for the day, as Mark enters. Through the screened partition, I watch as my brother pulls open the tool drawer and removes...a scissors. Mark's prank is immediately revealed and it becomes apparent that Brian's cost-saving effort, although recognized, will not be rewarded. With an impish grin, Mark carefully...artfully...snips off a small length, about an inch, from each of the already-too-tight apron strings, then carefully and delicately separates the threads at the fresh cuts to create a worn, frayed effect, thus eliminating any sign of his handiwork. The man is a perfectionist. The doors are soon locked and we leave for the night.

CHAPTER 6

GRANDMA
LEARNS TO DRIVE

SUNDAY 5:30 A.M.

MARY'S ALARM GOES OFF, MERCILESSLY, VERY EARLY ON SUNDAY morning; she quickly does her early morning routine and slips silently out of the house, unnoticed. Soon, we will all be hearing our own alarms but, for a few minutes more, we can slumber in the sleep of the just - or, at least, of the extremely tired. She drives in the pre-dawn darkness to the restaurant in Mequon, where she begins the job of slicing and frying yet another thirteen bushels of peppers...thirteen bushels! She uses the large institutional range, with gas-fired burners, which allows her to keep three very large pans going at the same time. Slicing, frying, slicing, frying - and so it goes until all fourteen bushes are lightly fried and refrigerated in large plastic tubs to await our pick-up on the way to the fairgrounds around eight a.m. My sister-in-law is one of the unsung heroes of Mille's Italian Sausage. Like most of the other

Mille women, they work very hard, often behind the scenes, in the offsite pepper frying operation as well as in the kitchens of the two stands. Mary, her daughter Megan, my other sister-in-law Donna, Toni, and the Mille women before them - grandma and mom - all have suffered silently (well, suffered anyway) while Mike, Mark, and I get to work out front where the action is. Megan will be working the entire Fair and will pretty-much be stabbing sausages in the kitchen all day long with her fiancé, Nick. (This real-life metaphor seems to go by unnoticed by Nick who shows neither discomfort nor any inclination to reconsider his future.) They'll be spending so much time together, side by side, in the kitchen making sandwiches: stabbing, stuffing, wrapping - hour after hour, day after day, talking to each other constantly, that one wonders if they will run out of things to discuss even before they're married. Probably not - they always seem to find fresh subject matter. Nick, while working in the kitchen, provides all of us with insights from his vast storehouse of arcane knowledge, should we need it. We call him Cliff from time to time.

Megan's and Mikey's sister Melissa, the one I used to be able to nose-flick, is also engaged and lives in Chicago now. She won't be working this year but she and her fiancé Frazer will visit. Since they were old enough to walk all of my brother's children and my own kids from my first marriage - Therese, Jennifer, and Matthew - spent every day, every year at the Fair. Once they were each tall enough to stand on a box and reach the soda dispenser they all helped out by pouring Cokes, under the watchful eye of their grandfather who was sure to nip-in-the-bud any over-filling tendencies they might exhibit. As they grew up, each of them assumed additional responsibilities and accumulated their own State Fair memories.

1956

"Mille's Bar-B-Q" is what the sign up on the roof states. It's a
misnomer in that we don't serve barbeque at all. In fact, in this year
of 1956, few here in the Milwaukee area have ever had barbeque -
real, southern-style barbeque that is; heck, grandma and my parents
just spent a number of years pioneering pizza pie and dealing with the
customer's disappointment when they weren't served a dessert. I think
the reason our family restaurant here on 82nd and Greenfield Avenue,
directly across from the State Fair, is named "Bar-B-Q" is because that's
the common term for what in later years will simply, and more accurately, be described as a charcoal grill. Dad included the construction
of such a grill, a very large one, in the center of the dining room. It has
a large stainless steel capital M, with a sweeping flourish to it, attached
to the middle of the chimney half way up to the ceiling. The grill was in-
tended to be the focal point where grandpa would grill Italian sausages,
although in a traditional horizontal grill fashion. But grandpa wasn't
up to the grind of grilling every day and it quickly has become just an
architectural feature. The State Fair is the place to get a Mille's sausage
and here, at the Bar-B-Q, pizza has been the main attraction since the
place opened in 1947. But during the Fair, it is also the place where
mom spends a lot of time frying peppers while grandma, for the most
part, either runs the restaurant or works in the stand at the Fair. Our
mother also spends many hours, again in the background, putting-up
the sharp peppers in large gallon jars (rather than frying them). This is
a secret pickling process that we will continue until 2003 when Wisconsin state inspectors enforce the law prohibiting restaurant usage of such
home-preserved products. But, until then, mom and later generations,
particularly the women, perform this tedious task of preparing sharp
peppers for the next year's Fair.

Mikey, Nick, Megan, Mary
and Mike

Grandma working hard – 1971

Grandpa telling Walter stories
about Italia

The State Fair is very crowded today and there will soon be a crisis at hand. Mom and dad are at the fairgrounds tending to the sausage business while I and my brothers are across the street here at the Bar-B-Q. I don't know for sure but I'm guessing that Toni, who will turn fourteen in a few months, is hanging out at the Little Theatre.

We're here so we can help grandma, who's primarily taking care of the restaurant, by flagging down drivers who are looking for parking spots. We have a small parking lot next to the restaurant and we can make some nice money by taking advantage of it. We've been standing at the corner where the traffic is heavy waving sticks and yelling "Parking...Parking...." I'm kind of taking the lead since I'm twelve and Mike is only eight. Mark, the youngest, is with grandma in the kitchen. It's meatball day - the day grandma prepares and fries-up a huge batch of meatballs for the next few day's pasta dishes. The smell of the frying meatballs, each with lots of garlic, is tempting; she's got a huge cast-iron frying pan loaded with them and I snitch one every chance I get. Grandma pretends to be annoyed but, with her old-country upbringing, she is glad to see her grandchildren eating a lot. The only other treat that I enjoy more is when she is frying fatback and gives me a plate of the crispy, fried little morsels. When she watches me wolf these down - she doesn't make them very often - she smiles and makes a little gesture; she holds her right thumb and index finger to the corner of her mouth and makes a slight twisting motion which is one of those unique southern Italian hand signals. This one means "tastes really good" or something along those lines. She uses her other, similar expression, when something tastes smooth and goes down the throat easily; as she tilts her head back, she strokes the front of her throat area and says something that sounds like "leesche" then translates that to "smooood" (as in "smooth") for us. Words like 'leesche", "fatti chiù cà" (move over a bit; give me some room to sit next to you) and "bă-cows" are a few of the Italian words we kids have picked up from grandma and grandpa, including of course, certain words and expressions that we know, just from the tone of their delivery, we should never repeat. But this list has been reduced since "bă-cows[17]", always understood to mean the bathroom or toilet as in, "pardon me, where's the bă-cows"?" has recently been exposed as not true Italian. This came about just last year in 1955 when grandma, dad and Toni went to Italy to re-unite with grandma's relatives who operate a small olive orchard business in Pomarico. At some point grandma herself, having eaten too many green olives, asked where the "bă-cows" was. After blank stares and quick discussion (including both words and gestures), the relatives finally figured out what she meant. The fact was that "bă-cows" is not an actual Italian word but simply an Italian-American immigrant's attempt to say "back house" as in privy or outhouse, the little shed with the crescent moon shaped cutout in the door that everyone older than a certain age was familiar with. It seems that, over the many years they've been in the U.S., grandma and grandpa, and presumably many other Italian immigrants, have forgotten they were actually saying "back house" - and how were the rest of us supposed to know? "Bă-cows" sounded Italian to us.

Anyway, grandpa is in the restaurant too. He's been sitting at one of the tables eating a sheep's head - not the fish, the actual wooly thing - which is on a plate in front of him. Of course, the wool has all been skinned off and its been roasted but it's a big old sheep's head none-the-less, glaring eyeballs and all. It seems to have an expression that can best be described as, well... surprised. This, too, is an unusual treat bestowed on grandpa by one of his meat suppliers, probably after re-

---

17   Correct spelling unknown, for a good reason, as will soon be made clear!

peated requests.[18] *Grandpa always preferred the unusual cuts of meat; at home, whenever mom roasts a whole chicken and after everyone else feasts on the breast, wings and drumsticks, he'll just put the remaining carcass, mostly bones and gristle, on his plate and pick off whatever he can salvage...nothing wasted. Then he'll tell me that the remaining bony shell is "...my boat... imma gonna ride-a de ocean back to Italia...." I thought this picking over the carcass was an act of great sacrifice and only recently have come to realize that the meat found there, though small in quantity, is pretty darn good...way juicier and tastier than the breast meat.*

Now, here at Mille's Bar-B-Q, he has his gallon jug of home-made red wine on the floor next to him and has been offering a friendly drink and conversation to the locals who stop by to visit with him (never mind the fact that we have a full-service bar in the adjacent cocktail lounge). He even offers a glass to the local cops who stop by to say hi and he can't understand why they politely decline. Just as at home, and as he did in Bari, he drinks his wine from a water tumbler, never from an actual wine glass. The parking lot is finally full, very full, so I've now joined grandpa at his table, just a few feet from the Wurlitzer. While I play SIXTEEN TONS *and* CHERRY PINK AND APPLE BLOSSOM WHITE *over and over, two big hits from last year that I won't let dad take off the juke box, he tells me, again, about some Italian guy he calls King Umberto and how great a person he was.*

"Amatore, I'ma tell-a you bout-a King Umberto. Himma wasa king of Italia; wasa gooda man; himma looka lika god I'mma tella

---

18   In testimony to the adage of the "apple not falling far from the tree", even one generation removed, I myself have been taking little tins of anchovies, pilfered from the Bar-B-Q storage room, to school with me from time to time. There, I enjoy my little snack of salty, pin curled anchovies on the recess playground while all the other kids are eating Twinkies or Sno Balls and the like. They look at me as if I'm eating a sheep's head!

you!; bigga mustache like-a dis" he says as he strokes a huge, imaginary mustache that must have been something-to-see. His description of this Umberto guy's noble appearance I can only associate with his pride of Italy and all things Italian. In later years, he will take me downtown to see the live telecasts of the two Carmen Basilio - Sugar Ray Robinson fights at the big movie theater there. He will cheer loudly every time Basilio lands a punch, which won't be all that often especially in the second fight, and will remind me that Basilio, like us, is Italian, just in case I'd forgotten. Secretly, I will admire the style and skills of Robinson but will not, cannot, reveal this and will be careful to not react when Sugar Ray dances around the lumbering Basilio, artfully setting him up with jab after jab before delivering a flurry of combinations. I, of course, will be aware that, years earlier, Robinson had taken the crown away from another Italian, Rocky Graziano. T<small>HAT</small> is a sensitive subject!

Grandpa's retelling of the greatness of Umberto is broken by the appearance of a woman and her two small kids who have come into the restaurant to let us know there's a car blocking hers. Mike and I go out to the lot and, sure enough, it's that last car that grandma insisted on squeezing into the lot that's preventing the woman from pulling her Buick sedan out. The car is a white Porsche convertible, the kind that looks kind of like a bathtub turned upside down. Really nice. It's owned by a dentist who knows grandma and grandpa pretty well. He comes in every so often for lunch with one of his assistants. I remember them because the blond assistant is really attractive and, although just twelve, I'm beginning to notice these things. With such a huge crowd at the Fair today all of the lots are full, including ours, but the dentist convinced grandma to let him park behind the Buick and left his keys with us, just in case. I guess he assumed the bartender or dad would be around to move it if necessary, but they're not. The bartender doesn't get here till four p.m. and dad's in the park. The Buick-lady is eager to leave with her kids who obviously have had a long day at the Fair and are in desperate need of a nap. She asks us, again, to move the white car, the Porsche, so she can get going. She tells us she would be happy to move it herself but can't drive a stick shift. The only other adults around are grandma and grandpa. Never mind the stick, neither of them has ever driven a car...period. But grandma, never one to be intimidated by a lack of education or experience, looks at this as just another thing she has to learn - quickly. Up to this point - and I'm not making this up - her only driving experience was on the back of a donkey in the rugged hills of her family's olive orchards near Pomarico, Italy. Retrieving the keys to the Porsche and walking out to the lot, she opens the car door and awkwardly plops down onto the driver's seat, her floral patterned housedress with its low neckline making it difficult for her to do this gracefully. Grandma always likes to dress very comfortably and almost always wears one of a number of very similar light cotton dresses. She's a medium height, strong woman, and the sleeveless dress reveals heavy upper arms that were made for, or perhaps by, heavy work. Large bosomed, she is most comfortable in loose fitting, unrestricted dresses, her always-present corset not withstanding. Grandma manages to get her legs into the narrow space and, after modestly adjusting her hemline, catches her breath, and forces the key into the ignition. Having often sat next to dad while he drove the family car, she begins to do the things that she has seen him do. She knows that one of the pedals on the left has to be pressed down and, after starting the car, slowly released. While I nervously look around, fearing the return of the dentist who, should he see this scene, will likely never return with the good-looking assistant...the Porsche begins to move slowly forward, the wrong direction, in herky, jerky starts and stops. The woman, with the grumpy kids hanging on her arms, tries to tell grandma how to move the stick shift into reverse - she's never done it either - and, after a series of dreadful, metal-on-metal grinding noises, the car begins to back up until the Buick is finally free to depart. I suspect the woman in the departing Buick has reservations about ever leaving her car with us in the future. The dentist, on the other hand, will never know of the details behind the moving of his white convertible and I will not be denied his occasional future lunch stops - with staff.

CHAPTER 7

THE DEATH OF
THE CISCO KID

SUNDAY 8:30 A.M.

LIVESTOCK TRAILERS ARE COMING AND GOING. WE'RE PULLING
into the 84th Street gate of the Fair and are reminiscing about dad's
State Fair quirks and famous moments. "Toni – make yourself look
small" jokes Mike, quoting one of dad's more outrageous demands.
We all laugh, remembering dad's half-kidding comment made in
this very spot many years ago. Half-kidding. He always liked to
start the day off by thinking he was getting a good deal and, if he
could confuse the ticket-taker into admitting an adult at a child's
ticket price, well, that day was off to a good start. One year it got to
the point where dad had an ongoing battle with one of the ticket
takers and I'm quite sure dad was keeping score; it helped to have
a lot of people crammed into the car, made it tougher to count
the arms and legs. Mary will come to the park later today after
recovering from the pepper frying; the tubs of peppers that she

fried early this morning are in the rear of our car. Mark and Donna are waiting for us when we pull up at the big stand.

Brian arrives just as we begin to unload the peppers. He is cheerful and helpful as always. I intentionally hang around a bit longer than usual just to watch him put on the apron...his still-clean, recently altered, apron. He eventually grabs it off of his personal nail and Mark, Mike and I watch out of the corner of our eyes as he begins to tie it. He cinches it tight and we hear a muted curse that sounds like "Ahhh - damn"...but nothing more. However, it's only Sunday and there are still seven days and lots of tasty temptations ahead - and a handy scissors. I set-up the coffee and head over to the small stand with Toni as Brian stores his food from home on his refrigerator shelf and grabs a day-old cannoli from the fridge.

Toni and I have walked over to the small stand. Our morning staff is all here and Toni is busy cleaning up the kitchen and directing them in their own clean-up of the counter tops and other areas outside of the kitchen. I'm cleaning the cash register of the previous day's ash and soot. There's lots of it. Last night, when I showered, I experienced the smell sensation unique to Fair week that can be best described as wet, smoky hair. It only lasts for a couple of seconds when the shower spray first hits my head. By the time I've applied shampoo the odor is gone and I feel normal again. If today were the last day I worked at Mille's and, one day, far in the future, I were exposed to that smell I am sure I would be flooded with State Fair memories, so unique is the odor, and so strong its association with the Fair.

1979

The plains of western Canada are magnificent. Chuck and I are putting miles behind us. He's driving and I'm in awe of the rolling prairie of western Saskatchewan. The very name itself, "Saskatchewan", stirs within me many rich, but arms-length associations with hunting and fishing adventures, all experienced in my imagination and through the well-detailed stories of OUTDOOR LIFE and FIELD AND STREAM magazines. As I look out across the vast, undeveloped landscape I think, too, of the plains Indians and how they must have lived and traveled in these lands. There, where that small stream meets the larger river just below the big bend, on the high bank, that is a place I would love to explore for signs of their occupation in ages past; a piece of chipped flint, a round stone with one of it's edges, which ought to be smooth, pecked away – perhaps even a whole projectile point – a spear point, I would guess, since these were the buffalo lands. We are a long way in distance and time from the Indian Mound of the Wisconsin State Fair of my youth but my feelings of excitement, hope, and the desire to search, at this moment, are really not all that different from when I first saw that small knoll. But we do not stop. We have a deadline to meet and Calgary, Alberta is still many miles ahead.

2000

I have gone through most of the boxes in my parent's basement at our family home on 88th Street. We're all in town for Christmas this year of 2000; mom has asked Toni, Mike, Mark and I to go through the accumulation of old family stuff in the basement and take what we want. There is still one group of boxes to go through and I begin to dig into them. I uncover a couple of old circular aluminum pizza trays from Mille's Bar-B-Q, grandma's original restaurant and I decide to hang onto them as a keepsake. Digging deeper, I pull out a few old cloth napkins and, there, hidden beneath them, is a memento of my youth that I had forgotten about many years ago. But I am instantly inundated with State Fair memories as I look at the old brown leather bullwhip. It had been hidden here, by my mother (I'm certain of that) about 43 years ago to keep me from blinding myself or others. My basement cleaning efforts are put on hold as I pick up the old whip by its wooden handle, the leather now dry and cracked, and go back to that time...

1957

It's an August day in 1957 but it's not just another day at the fairgrounds and Richie and I have plans. A rodeo is going to be held over in the Coliseum, which in itself is significant, but in addition, the star of my favorite TV western, the Cisco Kid is supposed to be there. I have seen every episode of The Cisco Kid on our black and white television and can't wait to see him in person. I don't know if his trusty sidekick, Pancho, will be appearing as well, but that would just be frosting on the cake. The Cisco Kid and Pancho with their "Oh Pancho"... "Oh Ceeeeesco" are sort of a south-of-the-border version of The Lone Ranger

and Tonto ("mmmmm, Kemosabe") who I also enjoy. But my favorite is
*The Kid; he is more of what I want to be, swashbuckling like The Three
Musketeers, but in a cowboy sort of way. There's nothing understated
about The Cisco Kid. Even his black leather doublewide belt (so wide it
needs two silver buckles, upper and lower) brings attention to himself,
like one of those ridiculously huge championship belts that later-period
boxers will flaunt. And there's that contagious, broad smile, even when
he's shooting bad guys. The Lone Ranger, on the other hand is more like
me, stoic to a fault, hiding behind his mask. No, I want to be like the
Cisco Kid.*

It's late morning and I've already told mom I want to go to the
rodeo later in the day. She knows all about my love of the cowboy life,
and, certainly, of the Cisco Kid; my breaking away will not be a problem. Well before the rodeo, however, Richie and I– we're both thirteen
years old and will be moving up to eighth grade at St. Anthony of
Padua next month – explore the fairgrounds, as is our routine. I've had
my eye on a bullwhip that I saw at one of the carnival souvenir stands.
This is no toy; it's a real, braided leather whip, about ten feet long with
a wooden handle and a long leather snapper-thing (that makes the
cracking sound) at the very tip. I know that mom, although always
generous, will not want me to have the whip for the same reason she
will not let me have a BB gun; she's afraid I'll shoot my eye out (her
exact words, just like the mother in the CHRISTMAS STORY movie of the
future) or, in this case, snap it out. This leaves me with just one resort.

"Grandpa – will you let me have $7?" I ask.

"Why you no aska you momma?" my grandfather asks curiously, his
kind, dark eyes searching my face for clues. He knows me well enough
to know that something's fishy. He's sitting in the family car parked
behind the stand where he had been taking a little nap. I lean on the
open window on the passenger side where he sits.

*"I want to buy something and she won't let me have it" I explain.
"I promise not to tell her you gave me the money" I volunteer, knowing what he's thinking. Grandpa always had money squirreled away.
We once found a roll of singles in an old shoe in the basement of our
house on 88th Street and one of my earliest memories is of seeing him
hiding something – it had to be money – behind a loose brick in the
basement of our first family home on South 10th Street. I guess he was
just protecting his nest egg; keeping it away from grandma since she
would only squander it on something foolish – like real estate. And
generous he was…earlier this past spring I had my heart set on a new
baseball glove that I had seen. It cost an unheard of price of $30 but I
wanted it badly. I had approached him in the solitude of our back yard
while he was putting in his tomato plants (no flowers for him, that
was grandma's thing) and asked him, pleaded with him. I'm sure that
even for an adult like grandpa it was a real sacrifice to come up with
the $30, but he did.*

*Now, digging his hand into his back pocket, grandpa pulls out his
old, well-worn leather wallet and, slipping a ten from it, he hands the
bill to me and holds his right index finger to his lips.*

*"Ssshhh" he says softly and a bit nervously. "Amatore, you go buy;
bringa backa change, no tella you momma".*

*I thank him and rush off down Grandstand Avenue where the
man selling bullwhips, along with actual children's toys, is set-up.
Upon arriving there I do the deal, no questions asked, and rush off
to see Richie behind the old wooden roller coaster, the Sky King, as
planned. There, we meet-up in the relatively open grassy area and
practice with the whip. A woman passing by with little kids give us a
motherly-glare…and shepherds her children around us in a very wide
berth. As they move away I hear her telling one of them, probably the
boy, why he can't have one of those, and glares back at us again. Not*

one to be intimidated by authority, Richie continues and, being a true hellion, is the first to get a good crack from the whip...but I soon get the hang of it myself.

A few minutes later, I have to use the restroom so we both go into the old, run-down, men's room that's right behind the roller coaster. It's dark and dingy in there and it appears that it's just the two of us but, as we're standing at the urinals, doing our business, we hear a deeply pained, grunting and moaning sound coming from our left. We both look in that direction and realize it's coming from one of the restroom stalls...and then we hear it again, even louder. Richie, never a shy kid, bends down and looks at the bottom of the line of stalls. He sees something and motions for me to take a look, just as a loud, heavy sigh comes from the same area. After looking nervously around to make sure no one is behind us, I bend down and take a peek. There, clear as day, is a pair of shiny black cowboy boots with silver spurs. I have barely risen back to a standing position when we hear the toilet flush. With our curiosity whetted, we go to the sink area and begin to wash our hands. Mom would have been pleased but I'm not really thinking of personal hygiene; we just want to hang out a minute or two to see who's in the stall.

The door to the toilet stall swings slowly open and, to our utter amazement out comes the Cisco Kid - Duncan Renaldo - himself! Our jaws drop in disbelief for, not only are we in the same men's room with the Cisco Kid, but we are looking at a man that could not be more unlike the TV star that we both idolize. Before us is a hunched-over, very tired looking old man with a cigarette hanging from his lower lip and a big paunchy gut where his fancy, wide belt ought to be. He makes no effort to look at us but quickly washes his hands and slowly shuffles out the rear door, stamping out the butt of his cigarette as he does so. In this brief encounter I have been shocked into realizing that there is no Cisco Kid. Not really. There is just a bored and tired actor, who, for a few minutes later this day, will put on a character and a show and will entertain a lot of kids. His shiny black doublewide belt will act as a girdle and he will, for those few minutes, support the fantasies of all his local fans. Richie and I will be there and we will see him ride out on his beautiful black and white pinto, Diablo, but it will not be the same, not even close. A little older and wiser, I will, nonetheless, enjoy seeing the real cowboys of the rodeo wrestle steers and ride bucking horses... and I will still want to be a cowboy when I grow up. But my days of enjoying a certain TV program and losing myself in its white hats versus black hats drama are a thing of the past. The Cisco Kid, for me, is dead.

1979

It's early July and I'm at the Calgary Stampede. My Tucson trip last spring was a mere tease for this world-class, western fair. Now, everything is ratcheted-up an entire order of magnitude. The crowd is huge and cowboy hats, real ones, are everywhere. The woman responsible for Stampede food concessions is very friendly and notices my enthusiasm at being here for the first time. She tells me about the wonderful trout fishing in the Bow River which cascades down from the mountains just to the west and meanders through the city itself before continuing on through the open prairies of Alberta. Her husband guides float fishing trips on those fast flowing, aqua green waters. I'm tempted...but realize that I have to hunker down and tend to business.

Chuck and I get our mobile unit set up and hire a crew of boys and girls but no sacrificial lamb. I make my way back to the administrative offices to see the concessions manager. She has invited me to join her backstage to watch the Plains Indian native dance competition that's about to begin. An authentic Plains Indian village is set-up right on the Stampede grounds and is temporarily inhabited by members of the Sarcee, Stoney, Peigan, Blood, and other tribes indigenous to the area. Teepees are everywhere and tribe members in authentic dress are living and mingling there.

I feel extremely privileged when we step onto the large open-air stage (in this case, "back-stage" actually means on-stage) and watch the dance competition. A dozen or more full-blooded Plains Indians in elaborate feathered dress whirl and step to the drumbeats. Beyond them, a large audience of Stampede attendees, mostly families, sits facing the stage. The Indian dress – never "costume" I am told – is handmade by each dancer. Hundreds of feathers, beads, porcupine quills, shells, and metal tinklers decorate most of the apparel on stage … and everything is magnificent. As I watch with great respect and awe, a single, small white feather floats off of a contestant's shirt and, becoming aware of it, the young man stops his dance and dejectedly moves to the side of the stage. He has disqualified himself since the loss of a single bead or feather from a contestants dress – pants, shirt, headdress, any part for that matter – is the basis for elimination. I can only wonder at his disappointment after what must have been hundreds of hours of painstaking work and many hours of practice. At the same time, I am amazed that any feathers remain attached at all considering the fast, furious pace of the dances.

The true spirituality of native peoples, like these Plains Indians of Canada, is something that I have always admired and felt an affinity towards. My experience here at The Stampede, seeing these people living close to their original ways, if for only about a week each year, is a huge fringe benefit of this venture of mine.

On the stage, between competitions, I am introduced to one of the officers of the Calgary Stampede. He wears a western hat and shirt in a way that clearly states this is not some "going-to-the-stampede" outfit. These are the kind of clothes he has worn all his life. They are second nature to him. I come to understand that he is a full-time cattle rancher in Alberta. Learning of my interest in such matters, he tells me that on his ranch there is a pre-historic buffalo jump, a place where a mesa ends in a cliff from which herds of stampeding buffalo would fall to their deaths as they were pursued by the Plains Indians. He extends an invitation to explore it but I can only thank him and wish I were in a position to accept the offer. This, for me, is one of the most appealing invitations that I will ever be offered and it is extremely difficult to turn down. I might as well have been asked, as a young boy, to help dig into the Indian Mound at the Wisconsin State Fair.

Getting back to work at the sausage wagon, business has been excellent and, just as with Tucson and Winnipeg, there is a great deal of interest in dad's vertical charcoal grill and the wonderful things it does to an Italian sausage. The kids I hired are all terrific and I will not have to fire any of them. Each of them has their own story and, with no family of my own around, they take the place of brothers and sister and teenaged children. Later, after little more than a week of working together there will be a certain melancholy in having to say goodbye, wishing them luck in school and other pursuits.

I've been working long, hard hours since the Stampede started and, on the 4th of July, just another day here in Canada, I see a small window of opportunity to take a half day off to explore the Canadian Rockies of Alberta. So after a hastily planned combination of bus, walking, hitchhiking, and strenuous mountain hiking I finally arrive at the top of a remote mountain ridge. I am looking down upon a glacial cirque which embraces a beautiful, sky-blue alpine lake. From this height I can see trout, probably cutthroats, cruising just below the surface. In every direction, I see nothing but mountains, small ponds, and alpine meadows. The Bow River, whose angry, crashing, upper reaches I crossed at the trailhead a few hours ago, is a slender thread of green far off to my right. It will eventually tumble its way out of the mountains and begin its fast glide into downtown Calgary, just below the Stampede grounds, before slowing down in its flattened meander across the Alberta prairies.

In this natural cathedral I find myself able to hear my soul and my God in ways I could never do at St. Anthony of Padua or any other church. The boulders of this rocky talus slope on which I sit are, for me, a better chapel than any man-made version constructed from similar stone enhanced with stained glass and mortar. Here, in this wilderness, I am unfettered of task lists and constant distractions. My deepest feelings and truths bleed-through to my conscious mind and I begin to understand the source of that vague, nagging, something's-missing feeling I experienced at the midway in Winnipeg just two weeks before. Dwelling on this for a while, I allow it to marinate on my mind. Feeling a bit more self-aware, I begin to think about getting back as a suddenly cold wind reminds me that I have a long hike out of here. The weather can get bad in a hurry at this altitude.

1973

"How many miles left?" I ask an anxious customer whose hanging binoculars peg him as a car race fan who has just exited the stands to grab a bagful of sandwiches. It's a race day in 1973 and we're about to get blasted.

"Only about thirty when I came out just a minute ago" he says with a smile, hurriedly pocketing his change and quickly walking away with his sandwiches.

"Amatore, do you have enough fire? Better get ready; big push coming" - dad is looking at me with an expression that says he's concerned

that his twenty-nine year old son will fall behind. His worry is justified; when the race ends thousands of fans will pour out of the stands and many will rush directly to Mille's for a sausage sandwich. Business is brisk right now but in a few minutes they'll be three and four deep along our entire front and sides with every one of them waving a cash-filled hand trying to get their order taken. It's no time to run out of sausage but it's been getting busier and tougher to keep up every year. Ten minutes later, I dump another full bag of charcoal, bringing the coals right up to the brim of the grill. There's a slight breeze from the southeast and, within a few minutes, I've got tremendous heat. Now, just as the emerging race crowd attacks our stand, I'm slapping spits of sausage onto every open spot on the grill – front and back, top to bottom. Five minutes later, as quick as I can move, I'm sliding cooked sausages off of spits into the old Nesco warmer and the women in the kitchen are forking them out and making sandwiches, also as quickly as they can; before I can even replace the cooked spit with a raw spit they're calling out "more sausage!" and I frantically jockey the spits around on the grill like a guy playing hide the pea. It's a chess game played at super-speed and I'm trying to plan three to four moves ahead, always seeking that elusive, constantly shifting, hottest spot for my next spit while guessing at which of the others will be ready after that, and thus worthy of the second and third hottest spots, which are also constantly changing and moving. Dad's ringing up sales and making change and looks over... "Amatore, put another spit on" and I tell him I'm cooking as fast as I can and I notice that the waitresses are having to act as referees, determining which person in the jammed crowd is actually next to be served – a situation of empowerment that is difficult and, for the most part, thankless. In the midst of all this, my wife Mary[19], who has been

---

19   My first wife. I now also have two children, Jack and Juliette, with my second wife, Margaret.

walking the fairgrounds with our three children, Therese, Jennifer, and Matthew, rushes into the stand; she's frantic. She tells me they were in the jam-packed Trade Mart building, just behind our stand, and someone snatched our youngest, Matthew, who turned two just a few months ago, and disappeared with him. "What do you mean? How did that happen...?"

Over the next few minutes, she describes a nightmarish experience when she and our young children had stopped to look at an exhibitor's coloring books. While asking our girls about the books, she had let go of Matthew's hand - for just a second - and in that instant... he was gone. She first looked under the table, expecting to see that he had crawled there, then she began to yell for him and for help from the people around her. A woman standing nearby asked if he was the little blond haired boy in the white shirt. She then says that, just a few moments ago, a man with a moustache picked him up...the man had a teddy bear. With that, my wife, understandably and appropriately, went berserk. She screamed for someone to call the police and looked for our son and the man in the extremely crowded building but with two other small children at her side she was unable to find the abductor who had quickly left, carrying our son; it had all happened so fast.

While still working the grill, never missing a flip of the spits, I attempt to calm her, to assure her that everything will be OK, that our young son will turn up unharmed and no worse for the experience - it's surely just some big mistake of some sort. Soon, the State Fair police and detectives are all over the situation - she had contacted them immediately. We get occasional updates from the detectives and wait anxiously.

1977

Four years have gone by since that dark afternoon in 1973, almost to the very day. Back then there was little publicity or awareness of child abductions. On summer days young kids ran around their neighborhoods playing with friends and exploring their world. When they got hungry or thirsty you'd see them, otherwise you just assumed they were safe, at least from other adults. That innocence is now lost.

I'm cooking again and, if anything, it's only gotten busier over this handful of years. My mother just returned here to the stand from yet another afternoon spent in the fairgrounds with her grandchildren and she has that huge smile she always wears when she's around them. She'll have stories to tell of their recent adventures with her. They've been off to whatever happens to be the newest attraction for children at this year's Fair. With her are Therese, Jennifer, Missy, Megan, Mikey and, of course, Matthew. He's become an adventurous, outdoorsy-kid with dirty-blond hair. He's also become nearly inseparable from me. We did get him back that day, four years ago in 1973, but only after hours of fear. It was a truly scary and near-tragic situation. Back then, a young woman was enjoying the Fair on that race-day afternoon, moving through the midway throng when a man with a moustache suddenly stepped in front of her and shoved a screaming young boy with a teddy bear into her arms saying, forcefully, "Here - you take him." He then disappeared, just as quickly, into the densely crowded amusement rides area. Within minutes she brought the boy to the Police Building. My wife was there talking with the detectives when they entered the building. She saw our son in the woman's arms and, just like that, our ordeal had ended. We will never know who the man was or why he took our boy but, every time I see a missing-child alert, I am reminded of that near-tragic day, which, thankfully, ended mer-

cifully, and I remind myself to not take my children, – any of them – for granted, to make the most of my time with them. Sometimes I forget and sometimes I get busy with life's distractions but I eventually remember. How could I not?

Leaving his grandmother's side, Matthew runs over to me, at the back of the stand, and I hear, "Daddy, will you take me on that ride now?" with pleading eyes looking up to me, knowing I'm on a break and this may be his last chance.

"Ohhh, Matty" I sigh, discouragingly, looking across Second Street and up at the monstrous swinging pirate ship that's been in nearly full view for the entire Fair. I'm about sick just from watching others, almost all teenagers, go on that insane carnival ride. It swings back and forth in an ever-increasing arc and eventually just hangs there, suspended upside down, with people screaming like they're about to die, till it eventually swoops down again to unload and take on a fresh boatload of willing victims.

"Pleeeease dad – while you're on your break, now?"

"All-right, just this one time" …and I've given in. The two of us quickly go off hand in hand across Second and make our way to the ticket booth. Within minutes we're being assigned a pirate ship seat, side by side, just the two of us, and I'm asking myself if I'm truly crazy but mainly wondering if this bar across our laps is really tight enough to secure such a small child, just over six years of age, when this whole thing is upside down and gravity is having it's usual effect. But the carnie with the dirty T-shirt who's operating the ride seems unconcerned and we're suddenly beginning to move. Nothing unpleasant yet; maybe it won't be so bad after all. Then, it becomes bad, after all. We've hit the apex of the arc and come to full stop. Upside down. People screaming. Since we first started to move I've had my arms around my son but now, with us hanging a hundred feet or so above the ground,

with everything confused and out of perspective, I am holding onto Matthew as hard as I can for I truly fear he could slip out and fall to a certain death. At the same time, I feel like crap, I'm nauseas, I'm mad at myself for agreeing to do this, but more than all that, much more, I am extremely frightened for the safety of my little boy. As I'm squeezing him I promise myself that I will not let him slip away; I am not going to lose this boy who means so very much to me, no matter what I have to do to protect him. Don't these people operating this damn ride know he could slip out? Why aren't they bringing us back down? I'm scared for my son, I'm angry that we're in this predicament, and more than anything, I'm NOT going to let go of him! An eternity has passed and, finally, thank God, the ship begins to move and we begin to swing down as I also promise...never again! On uncertain legs we make our way back to the stand where Mark and Mike ask me how it was. I can only shake my green-faced head, and take a seat. I wind up having to recline and close my eyes, hoping to not puke but really not caring all that much if I do. I eventually, about an hour or so later, feel better; the nausea has, by and large, passed. Reaching into the right pocket of my shorts, I realize the ten dollar bill, my change from the ticket booth, is missing; gravity is alive and well. The carnies operating the barf boat must make out OK with the involuntary tips they receive; they probably have a regular work schedule, a rotation, to equitably divvy-up their time working this money machine. Pennies from heaven; folding money too. Or maybe they have a seniority system in place, with the pirate ship being the real plum assignment, I don't know, but my sense of annoyance at the loss of the sawbuck is tempered by my relief at having that experience behind me and the nausea almost gone. More than anything, though, I am thankful that my son is now safe. In the future – but not today, not for a while – I will realize how irrational my fear was. Surely, he was in no real danger on that ride; those carnival rides

A busy fair day in the 1970s

Melissa and Matthew working
the "small stand" in their teen years

are all safety-checked every time they're erected. If there was real risk far more children, worldwide, would be getting hurt or killed than the extremely few that actually are. No, my fear was certainly unreasonable but, at the time, when we were up there hanging upside down, that bar looked and felt like it had far too much space between it and Matthew's lap and, at least in my head, the danger was real. Just four years ago he was really in harm's way, snatched from his mother's arms. How many children, under that circumstance, an actual abduction, are ever recovered safely? Fifty percent? Twenty-five percent? Fewer? I don't know but I'm sure they're pretty lousy odds compared to the millions-to-one ratio (in our favor) we faced up there on that ride. But, warranted or not, that ride did evoke very strong emotions from me and I'm just relieved and happy to have this boy still in my life.

EARLY 1980s

Dad is in State Fair mode again. He's a little nervous about the weather. Its been pretty hot, which hurts food sales - and even his humor now has an edge to it that is uniquely his, balancing precariously between pushiness and absurdity. He gets that way sometimes, especially when he's back in his element, here at the State Fair. His oldest grandson, Matthew, is on the cusp of childhood and teen years and had been working hard yesterday. Then he began to pass-out, almost fell to the ground. Matty was apparently suffering from heat stroke and was helped outside where he sat down to recover. He remained there for the rest of the evening and went home with us last night. We all hoped he would feel better by morning, for his sake, as well as ours, since we're short of help, and dad's got that edge going.

 It's early, next morning and the door to Matty's bedroom opens slightly...just a small crack.

"Matthew...are you awake?" his grandfather whispers softly through the opening.

"mmmmm... (yawn) ... Yeah, grandpa ... mmmmmm" he sighs sleepily, eyes still closed.

The door opens a few inches further.

"Are you feeling better?" his grandfather asks, his voice soft and probing.

"aahmmmm ... (big yawn, eyes opening)...yeah, grandpuba, I think so."

With the door now cracked open about a foot, "grandpuba" is peering in, his rather prominent nose, Romanesque as it is, leading the way.

"Are you ok? Can you go in this morning?" the concerned voice asks.

"mmmm...yeah, I guess so...yeah... (yawn)...OK."

The door now opens all the way and his grandpa is standing there, all dressed and ready to go in his boss-green Mille's Italian Sausage shirt.

"Well then get your ass out of bed and get dressed!" he fairly shouts with an exaggerated, stern expression on his face, worthy of any burlesque stage. But his countenance quickly softens and Matty, knowing his grandfather well-enough, is amused. At the same time though, he hops quickly out of bed, shakes the cobwebs, and rushes to get ready. Like I said, he knows his grandfather pretty well. In years to come he will retain this as one of his fondest memories of his "grandpuba"- my dad - at the Wisconsin State Fair.

Later that morning at the Fair, young teenagers are coming into the Lutheran Dining Hall for their morning shift. A couple of them, obviously not part of the regular morning crew, glance curiously at us, as if to say, "what are they doing in here? We don't serve breakfast."

And they don't…except to dad and his clan. All of the family, with dad at his throne, is seated at "our" table, a long picnic-style one. The rest of the large dining hall is full of long empty tables which won't seat customers till much later in the morning. The folks who run the Lutheran Dining Hall have our table set for us every morning, awaiting our arrival at about nine a.m. We go there right after we set-up our own stand. Dad had made an arrangement with them years ago and this has become our routine. The Lutherans, if anything, love routine and, like clockwork, our plates of fried eggs and ham arrive. The eggs are served Lutheran-style, over-easy (the yolks add too much color to the plate) and we eat our breakfast together as we tease each other about yesterday's and this morning's events. Matty gets his share of ribbing but we also bring up the time, years ago when young Carl, twelve years old, felt some unintended peer pressure when the Lutheran waitress worked her way along the table pouring coffee. "Black… black…black" had all been requested and when she got to him with the big pot, he simply went along with the trend. Only later did I realize he almost never drinks coffee and certainly never without cream and sugar, lots of it. But he felt like that was just the way we did it at the State Fair and wanted to be a part of the team. The waitress saw nothing unusual in a twelve-year old drinking coffee, black coffee; to her it might as well have been a tuna hotdish.

CHAPTER 8

A DOZEN
SANDWICHES TO GO

SUNDAY 1:20 P.M.

MIDDAY HAS SNUCK UP AND MADE ITS PRESENCE KNOWN. THE
streets are jam-packed with a wide cross-section of State Fair hu-
manity; everyone's eating something. Sitting at the register, I have
a good look at the passing masses. Many stop and have a sandwich.
Those that don't at least slow down and take a look when they feel
the heat radiating from the grill.

"Is it hot in there?" is the question the cook will hear about
twenty times each day. I've learned to be tolerant and respond with
a friendly "sure is" but there was a time when I wasn't quite that
cordial. That year it was particularly hot, high nineties as I recall. I
was getting the classic question even more frequently than usual,
so I made up a little handwritten sign. When the question was
asked, usually accompanied by a clever chuckle as if the guy was
the first to ever ask it, I'd just hold up the sign which, of course,

read "Yes – It IS Hot In Here!" Not everyone thought that was funny. Elvis songs are being covered, along with Roy Orbison numbers, by the afternoon band at the Budweiser Pavilion, just across the grassy mall from us. We'll hear material that is more contemporary when the evening crowd takes over in a few hours. I swear, you could wake me from a deep sleep, blindfolded, and I could tell you what time of day it is just by the music being played. By midweek we all know all the words to every song in each band's repertoire.

PSYCHOLOGY TODAY magazine has nothing on us. Being in this stand for so many hours has us finding ways to pass the time when things are slow. One of my recent pastimes has been to observe the different reactions of men and women when they stumble slightly on the raised sidewalk crack in front of the small stand. It's a very small obstacle, no one has ever fallen, but it tends to cause one to trip slightly. Almost without exception the females, of all ages, will look slightly embarrassed and then just brush it off and move along without even looking back. Most guys, on the other hand, especially those past the age of puberty, will stop dead in their tracks and, turning back, throw a "who do ya think you're messin' with?" glare at the offending one inch raised crack that had suddenly leaped up at them. With the men, and it pains me to admit this, it is never their own clumsiness that's the problem. And so the day goes.

With his usual cheerful smile, Brian has just returned from a break. I'm fortunate enough to happen to be back here at the big stand, having eagerly awaited his return. I'm not sure where he went off to but State Fair food almost certainly was involved. While he was out, Mark made another slight alteration to the apron strings. Brian's such a nice guy and a good worker, I feel a bit guilty about this…but the feeling soon passes as I watch from a discrete distance.

"Hey Nick, could you please toss me my apron?" Nick is in the kitchen area making sandwiches and talking with Megan. Since getting engaged, they've had lots of planning on their minds.

"No problem Brian…here you go."

"Thanks, pal."

Without further comment, the apron goes on and Brian reaches behind to grab the strings. Pulling them together in front and while trying to knot them, his facial expression betrays his dismay, not unlike the feeling I've sometimes had when stepping onto my bathroom scale for the first time after the Christmas-New Years holiday week. With his large hands finally succeeding at tying a very tiny bow in front, the apron is now so tightly wrapped around his waist that he, himself, looks a bit like an over-stuffed sausage.

"Brian, how do you keep that apron so clean?" I ask. "You should give Roy some lessons." He smiles proudly and tells me he'll probably get through the entire Fair with just one apron.

"That's great. I'd love to see that."

Grabbing another sandwich for myself (my apron strings are fine) I head back to the small stand again. This is about my fourth sandwich today and I wonder how many I could eat if I really tried. Yesterday we had two big farm boys from Indiana hanging around all day eating sandwiches and raving about them. They'd buy three or four sandwiches (each), walk away, than return an hour or so later. These guys looked like their round faces would be smiling back at you from Polaroid shots tacked to the walls of restaurants that challenge you to eat their entire 48 ounce steak or two-foot high ice cream sundae, or whatever. Late that evening I asked how many of our sandwiches they'd eaten. Laughing, they did some quick estimating and decided that one of them, the guy on the right - the smaller of the two but still a big fellow by any standard, had eaten about twenty-three sandwiches. Twenty-three! That's the most I've ever heard of anyone eating, even over a very long day.

1961

Business has been very slow this late evening and it's just grandma and us four kids holding down the fort. We waited for the usual big push following the fireworks at the end of the grandstand performance but tonight it was just a trickle. Now there are very few people still in the park and most of them finished eating long ago. The streets look unusually dark and lonely with the relative silence broken only by the distant sounds of a country band at one of the beer pavilions and the occasional bawdy shouts from over-indulged young men leaving the park in small packs, as young men and other predators often travel. Toni and I now have our driver's licenses' and we are all eager to give up the ghost and drive back home...get to bed, but we can't leave until grandma says she's ready to shut it down for the night.

Much later in life I will recall this evening while staying at a bed and breakfast on tiny, remote, Smith Island in the middle of the Chesapeake Bay. Smith Island, as small and isolated as it is, is the center of America's soft shell crab fishery. This simple cottage industry is the lifeblood of all Smith Island residents - men, women, and children of all ages. On Smith Island they live for and by the Chesapeake Bay blue crabs. I will spend the night at the modest cottage of an 80-year old widow. She will tell me about herself over the she-crab soup she is serving and will began to describe her late husband, who, like all men on Smith Island, went crabbing all day, every day of the season. "That man of mine would walk a mile for a crab." That says it all and when I hear her say that I will instantly think of this night at the 1961 State Fair when it seemed that grandma would work an hour to sell one sausage.

Grandma is standing patiently in the kitchen area waiting for us kids to shout out an order while a dozen or so forlorn sausages sit in the charcoal warmed brazier, keeping hot. I've been cooking tonight and I've already done the shake-down of the coals, so it's just grandma we're waiting for. But she is not about to close up as long as there is a sausage left to sell, never mind the fact that there's no one to sell it to. She stands, quietly, with a very slight smile not unlike that of the Mona Lisa but even more subtle, as if to say, "I have all night to wait and as long as there's money to be made I'm going to stay open." Our pleading is getting us nowhere when, out of the dark, cool, night a savior appears. It's a middle-aged man in a Milwaukee Braves jacket, big tomahawk across the front, who is friendly and jovial and tells us he wants a dozen sandwiches in a bag. Hallelujah! He wants six sweet and six sharp. "Put a few extra peppers on them will ya?" he asks with a big smile.

"No problem" all four of us say almost in unison. As grandma begins to make and wrap the sandwiches, with help from my eager sister, the guy tells us he'll have to come back in a few minutes to pay us...his wallet is in his car, way out in one of the Fair parking lots. Only after this night is over will I realize the oddity of walking around a Fair without your wallet and money...which is locked up in your parked car. In testimony to the power of wanting to believe that something is true, grandma and all four of us kids, agree to give this god-sent, cordial redeemer his bag of sandwiches, believing that he will reward our trust with a speedy return.

The cute
waitresses
all like Roy

Dad and Mike on a
slow day in the old
knockdown stand
– 1971

"Be right back" he says with an emphasis on the word "right" as he leaves with his double-bagged sandwiches, looking me straight in the eye all the while.

"OK, we're not going anywhere" my bother Mike replies not realizing how prophetic his comment will prove to be.

Dad was always great at spotting a con. Maybe it was his many years of running a bar that sharpened his skills but I was struck by both his alertness and his self-confidence in standing-down an attempted con. One day, just a year or two earlier, I saw him deal with a man who claimed he had been short changed on his sandwich purchase. I was working the grill in the big stand when I noticed a commotion at the cash register where dad sat. "You gave the girl a five" dad was saying rather emphatically as he looked directly at the man, in a light blue T-shirt, a pack of cigarettes in the breast pocket, standing at the counter. An argument ensued, with the man claiming that he had given the waitress a twenty. Dad pulled the guy's five dollar bill from the till and held it up to him as evidence of the transaction. The man persisted and dad approached him as the argument heated up.

"Give me the change for my twenty or I'm going to get a cop" the man threatened with impressive anger.

"Don't bother; I'll call one for you. I saw you flash the twenty then pay with the five." My father was wise to one of the oldest confidence tricks around. The man then quickly began to back down, said something to save face and walked away with his change for the five. Later, dad told me about the old trick. The customer has a big bill in his hand or on the counter or bar but he then switches and pays with a much smaller bill. When he claims that he paid with a bigger bill the off-guard bartender or waitress will then often recall seeing the big bill and assume that they, in fact, did shortchange the customer. It's a clever trick.

Unfortunately, dad is not here tonight and as we patiently await the return of the nice man with his wallet we gradually begin to realize, as fifteen minutes turns into thirty, that we, all of us including our usually business-savvy grandmother, have been had. While Toni, Mike, Mark and I accept this, grandma is still reluctant to throw in the towel. Whether it's her strong passion for profits or her reluctance to admit that she's been hoodwinked that keeps her hopeful of his return, I can't say. Eventually, however, she gives in and admits defeat and we lock up for the night. As for us kids, we would rather have had the sausages stolen outright, than having our precious sleep stolen as well.

SUNDAY 10:40 P.M.

"Hey Roy, did you ride your mom's bike into the park today?" Brian asks. Roy's head is bouncing up and down, chicken-like but faster, to the beat of some unheard song, his headset wire implying that the CD player is tucked into the back of his waistband. "Roy..." Brian says again while finally catching his eye. The earphones come off of the tan University of Wisconsin cap with the big, red, block W in the front, its visor almost black from several fair-years of handling by a charcoal-dirtied hand. After Brian repeats the question, Roy, smiling broadly, replies "no" - but if he wants, he "can borrow it tomorrow." Brian's tease is a reference to something that happened a few months ago at Milwaukee's Summerfest where they, along with Les, worked at Mike's stand, an operation somewhat similar to our family business here at the Fair. It was a classic incident of cook-on-cook violence, Les and Roy, mano e mano...

JUNE, MILWAUKEE SUMMERFEST

They were all amazed. A grown man, riding a girl's bicycle. This was too good to be true; something they could tease him about all day – all week, really. Roy made no excuses, just laughed it off. "It takes a confidant man to ride a girl's bike" he said, and that was true, especially around this crowd – Mike, Brian, and Les – especially Les. An explanation was offered; he stayed at his mom's house last night. She lives close to the grounds and it was a lot easier to ride the bike, her bike, than to deal with parking a car. Anyway, yes, it was a girl's bike…but it was blue. That probably made sense, but it wasn't good enough for them. No, Roy had shown a soft underbelly and they were going for it. They teased him all day and he kept firing zingers back at them - good ones, too - but they were relentless. It didn't matter to him, he kept to his guns and rode the skirt-friendly bike the next day as well.

But something happened that second day to cause them to stop with the bike razzing; maybe they just got tired of it or maybe they felt they had pushed him far enough. In any case, they relented and moved on to other things. So, rather than bicycles, the conversations were focused on the current Brewers season as well as their mutual hopes for the Packers this fall. That second night, at closing time, Roy was eager to get back to his mother's home, hop in the shower, and catch a few minutes of Sports Center. With the stand closing down and him dead tired, he went out back to unlock the bike. A part of him, undoubtedly, was glad to no longer be their target, at least, not today and especially not tonight, he just wanted to get some sleep. Anyway, the bicycle really wasn't such a big deal. Yes, it was a girl's bike but the average person wouldn't even notice the subtle difference in the frame and no one except his buddies with too much time on their hands had made anything of it.

As he walked out the door of the stand, he stopped dead. There was the bike, barely recognizable. He now understood the real reason behind today's peaceful lull - it was merely the calm before the perfect storm. The bike now showed signs of someone's bicycle maintenance skills... and it had Les's stink all over it. Roy was shocked but he had no options, no contingency plan. Cursing was involved and even Roy's considerable self-confidence was tested as he biked off, through the grounds, past dozens of beer-brazened, jeering, young men. He could partially hide the pink Cinderella seat - at least the red hearts - but the hot pink handlebar streamers, the pink Little Princess handlebar bag, squeeze-bulb horn, and, the coup de grace...bright pink Barbie training wheels...could not be concealed. What was a short ride to his mother's house seemed infinitely longer that night.

SMALL REGRETS

FRIDAY 3:40 P.M.

WE'VE MADE IT ALL THE WAY TO FRIDAY AND, THROUGH SOME odd perception of time, although the days have been interminably long, the week itself has flashed by leaving me to wonder, in amazement, where the week went. It being the end of the work week for normal folks, I've checked in with my office and was glad to learn nothing urgent had come up in the past few days; it would be difficult to change mode this far into the Fair...better to just wait to the end.

Mark has continued to trim Brian's apron strings ever so slightly - just enough to make the apron a bit tighter each day. Brian is waiting for us when we arrive at the big stand this morning. He's brought in a salad, albeit a large one. We're all starting to feel more than a little guilty. It will be an entire year before Brian will have another chance to enjoy State Fair food and it really isn't right.

He's stowed his healthy lunch in the walk-in and is now donning his well-used apron. His fingers struggle to tie a knot and, after a few seconds of trying, he gives up and just ties the darn thing in the back, with plenty of string to spare now that he's finally given up on the wrap-around. Suddenly, it's a brand new ballgame.

It being a Friday, I have to figure out my fish fry strategy. Having lived in both Michigan and Pennsylvania since the late 70's I have come to realize that the Friday night fish fry is pretty-much a Milwaukee event, as much a local phenomena as is the bubbler thing. After being absent over twenty five years, I still occasionally, maybe once every five years or so, find myself almost slipping and asking someone - "where's the bub…, ahh, I mean, …drinking fountain?" It's deeply ingrained and pure-Milwaukee, just like the Friday night fish fry. I would love to get away for an hour or two and find a nearby tavern with a really good fish fry, lake perch is what I want, and maybe even get in an electric bowling game, the one with the heavy sliding metal puck that slides so easily over the cornmeal spread on the lane. But I can't figure out how I'm going to swing that so I'll probably just go to the Door County Fish Boil place; they'll have a decent fish fry of some type tonight. My favorite draft horses, the Percherons, are also on the fairgrounds now. They, along with the Belgians, started to take over the horse barns yesterday. I'll try to get a few minutes strolling there and maybe even get in ten minutes of the hitch competition. I always admire the power and beauty of these tar black, or occasionally dapple gray, behemoths with their immaculate braided manes and Shinola polished hooves. Their tails are often done up in a French-braid sort of style that seems appropriate for these draft horses from the province of Le Perche. At the hitch competition, young men and women in various types of shiny carriages will drive their

Percherons through the required routines. Whenever I watch this
I usually, for just a few moments, fantasize on the life of a horse
breeder and imagine living that sort of life. It's that old cowboy
thing of mine, still there after all these years, and no passing of
years or disappointing sightings of paunchy TV idols can seem to
put it to rest.

They're here, the Patrick Cudahy Barbershop Quartet. Frank,
John, Tom, and Bob have stopped by again this year. It's their day,
one day each year, to walk around the fairgrounds serenading fairgoers on behalf of their sponsor (the rest of the year they're the "All
In Accord Barbershop Quartet"). The Patrick Cudahy Company
is a local manufacturer of bacon, hams, and similar meat products,
which explains the way they're dressed - in matching old-time
country butcher outfits. It's another hot, very sunny day and they
look uncomfortably warm. Their Styrofoam "straw hats" keep the
sun out of their eyes, to at least some degree, but the heavy bright
yellow butcher's aprons must make them pretty warm on a day
like today. The beads of perspiration on their foreheads confirms
this. Walking up to me at the side counter, where I'm sitting at the
till, we exchange hellos and pleasantries; they're just as outgoing
and friendly as always and we all start to get updated on things
since last year's Fair, but we all know they're not really here to
see me and I take no offense in that knowledge. John, he's the
big guy (whose apron strings I'd love to trim), begins to scan the
kitchen area and, after his darting glances fail to find their target,
asks about my sister.

"Is Toni around today?"

"Yeah, she's in the back room; she'll be out in a moment."

The guys order sandwiches and we continue our little chat until Toni comes out to hugs all-around. I'm back to keeping my eyes

on the grill and the cash register and, before I know it, the singing starts as the four men join in perfect harmony:

"Lida Rose, I'm home again Rose, to get the sun back in the sky;
Lida Rose, I'm home again Rose, about a thousand kisses shy..."

As they continue, I recall how this all started. I had originally asked them to sing Lida Rose when I first saw them standing near our stand a few years ago. I love this sappy but beautiful song. I think I had recently been watching The Music Man musical on TV and it was fresh in my mind. Anyway, back then, when they finished singing, Toni, who was listening to them with me, asked if they were aware there was a female reply in Lida Rose. Through the ensuing discussion the guys found out that my sister is an accomplished professional singer and, being barbershop guys, well, they just love to sing and love people who share their love of music. Without a lot of prompting - my sister never needed much - they had quickly agreed to the right key or whatever it is that musicians figure out and the quartet sang and then she sang, and when she sang their eyes opened wide and they knew they were not listening to just another hot dog vendor. Since that day Toni and the quartet have had a little jam session each year right here at the small stand

The quartet finishes, their voices softly tapering away:

"Lida Rose oh won't you be mine?
Lida Rose...oh Lida rose... oh Lida Rose"

And Toni begins to sing. Suddenly, all of the kids working in our stand are startled by the voice coming from their boss. Most

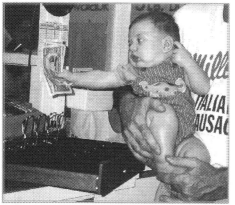

Author's son Jack
learning early

Brian showing off
his calves...again

Toni and the
barbershop quartet

of the customers within hearing range, which in her case, is most of this end of the fairgrounds, also look around for the source of the female voice:

"Dream of now, dream of then"
"Dream of a love song, that might have been..."

She continues, then softly finishes and we've all had our fix for the year. It's yet another part of our Fair tradition, a new element, for sure, but one that I look forward to. As for the kids in the stand, they seem to have a new respect for their boss. Although this may not be their style of music, they are beginning to see there's a lot more to Toni than just the super-organizer that keeps the small stand running so efficiently. I hear one of them asking her about her singing a few minutes after we've said farewell to the quartet for another year.

1979

Canada Highway 2 North stretches ahead and we've been driving in a steady stream of carnival ride traffic for a couple of hours with about one more to go before Edmonton. It's a short haul to the Klondike Days exposition grounds; most of the carnies left Calgary early this morning rather than last night, as did we. This highway must look like a modern version of an old time circus train except that, instead of circus wagons with elephants and calliopes, this "train" consists of semi-trailers with a collapsed Tilt-A-Whirl, Music Express, Fun House, and, this year, an Italian Sausage Wagon. About an hour back we passed a broken-down carousel truck; memories of an icy night in Texas. We've got a CB radio in the cab and we're occasionally hearing from passing truckers asking if we can hand them a sausage sandwich – yuk, yuk. All part of life on the sausage circuit in 1979.

We eventually make our way into the town of Edmonton and city traffic is heavy as we try to find our way to the Northlands Park site of the exposition. Somehow, we've managed to get onto a bridge over the North Saskatchewan River in downtown Edmonton but, thank God I saw the warning sign, there isn't enough overhead clearance for our rig. With traffic backing up behind us, I hop out of the cab and look behind to see a stream of Monday morning traffic waiting patiently (but that could change). I'm immediately both panicked at the dilemma facing us and relieved that I'm not at the wheel of the truck, faced with the need to back it and the trailer off that bridge, with a large, involved audience watching. God knows, I'd struggled backing up my twelve foot duck boat trailer on the Horicon Marsh ramp at five a.m. with no one but my duck hunting buddy Ken and a promising young lab named Sam critiquing my driving skills. Walking back along the line of stopped cars I nervously motion for them to back up so we can do the same. Amazingly, not a single horn blasts nor do I catch any annoyed glares. With a minimum of difficulty, all of the cars back up off the bridge and Chuck manages to get our rig out of this jam. Meanwhile, I'm just thankful we aren't in some place like Chicago or

New York – that would be ugly.

Eventually, we find a way to cross the river and make it to the Klondike Days grounds where we quickly locate our assigned spot and set up the sausage wagon. This venue is particularly stressful since it's our last operation in Canada this season and we can't readily cross back into the States with any remaining sausage inventory. The customs restrictions are just too daunting. At the same time, we don't want to run out of sausage halfway through the Exposition. What's a vendor to do?

In moving from Calgary to Edmonton we've left behind a cowboys and Indians culture and entered the world of the gold rush, hence the very name of this exposition. Gone are many of the cowboy hats; here the theme is gold pans, picks, and shovels. I am struck, too, by the size of the Ukrainian population and their presence here at Klondike Days. After I become familiar with the scene, one of my favorite food stops becomes the Pierogi stand run by local Ukrainians. This dumpling-like food of uncertain European origin is claimed by numerous nationalities; Russians, Latvians, Czechs, and, of course, the Poles all challenge the Ukrainians to the birthright of this morsel but here, in Edmonton, the Ukrainians rule. Their concession stand is staffed by Ukrainian women, old and young, whose Eastern European features authenticate the Pierogis they serve. The Pierogis, peasant food for sure, are good and I eat a lot of them.

When the Exposition finally opens we see the

usual level of interest from the locals who ask about
the charcoal grill and, in many cases, try a sandwich.
The week drags along slowly and our nights are spent
at a nearby inexpensive motel where our second level
room faces other wings of the motel, all surrounding a
central parking lot in a horseshoe shape. There is a regular little community of concessionaires staying here.
I've seen a number of them in Winnipeg and Calgary.
Chuck and I get in late each night after closing up and,
for the most part, we and the other concessionaires are
all quick to turn out the lights; 7 A.M. will be here too
soon. But there is one small group, just catty-corner
from us, that seems to party all night, every night.
The noise from their radio and shouting is truly annoying and it cuts into my sleep. To make matters
worse, Chuck and I have been getting on each other's
nerves. We've been sharing hotel rooms and the very
tight quarters of the sausage wagon for quite a while
now and even most married couples would need some
breathing room. Little things are setting us off and, to
make matters worse, he's a confirmed bachelor who
has always lived alone and has very precise routines.
My wet towel hung over the shower curtain rod gives
him angina and he and I have words. The honeymoon
is over for us.

Eventually, as the Exposition approaches its final
days, I take a careful count - an "honest count" - of
our remaining sausage inventory and determine that
we're overstocked. Not wanting to have to dump it at
customs, I decide to begin selling it in bulk at whatever

price I can get. A couple of handwritten signs are hastily made and I begin to offer bulk sales, in five-pound boxes at what was essentially our cost. Sales of both sandwiches and five-pound boxes are brisk and I begin a balancing act to make sure we don't cannibalize our sandwich revenues. On the last day, late in the day, we still have a few boxes left and a fellow asks if he can buy a couple. "Sure", I say. Then I tell him the price per box.

"OK; I'll take two but I'll have to come back with the money. My wife's got my wallet."

Anxious though I am to get rid of my excess inventory, he had just said the wrong thing to a man who still remembered a late, cold night at the Wisconsin State Fair in the 1960s when his grandmother refused to call it a night as long as a dozen sausages remained unsold. No, I'm not going to fall for it again.

"Sorry, but I have to get paid first."

"Hey, you can trust me; I'll be right back with the cash" then, apparently thinking it would influence me, he adds, "I'm a doctor."

Now, this leveraging of his Hippocratic Oath might work with my sister. Years ago, the whole carload of us were pulling into the driveway at mom and dad's in a loud, giddy, punch-drunk mood after closing up at the fairgrounds - it might have even been the very night of "grandma and the bag of sandwiches man" as we would forever refer to the incident. She, since it was very late and the neighbors' houses were all darkened, said, in a very reverent, hushed tone, while nodding towards the

neighbor's house to the left of our driveway "…Shh-
hhh – he's a doctor". Well, all of us admire and respect
doctors as much as the next person but that sort of
special consideration seemed a bit too much and, being giddy, we teased her about it then and remind her
of it frequently. So now, I'm dealing with a doctor who
feels that he should be given special consideration and,
as much as I'm tempted, I refrain from giving him a
smart-ass reply and simply tell him I can't make an exception. Although he leaves with an air of professional
indignation, he returns later and closes the deal.

Edmonton is wrapped up and we've gotten rid of
our inventory without a loss. It's been a very good first
year of operations in Canada and there is no question
that this can be a financially viable venture. The lifestyle
is quite another issue, however, and I've been thinking
about my dad's comment a few years ago, "sawdust in
your veins", he had cautioned. Dad was right. There
is a big price to pay in taking Mille's Italian Sausage
across North America. I haven't been home to see my
wife and kids since early June and we still have a couple
of big eastern fairs to go before our season is over. By
that time, summer vacation will be over, my children
will be back in school, and I will not have been able to
enjoy any part of the summer with my family. All of
this, along with my thoughts from a mountaintop two
weeks ago, is hanging heavily on my mind as we retrace
our journey across Canada. Moving south, boreal for-
ests become high plains and foothills. Then, eastward-
ly, vast rolling prairies dominate. Grain elevators, tall

and skinny, rise here and there, exclamation points on
the vast solitude. Wearily, we pull the sausage rig into
the parking lot of a roadside motel in Swift Current,
Saskatchewan, a town I had heard of from the pages of
OUTDOOR LIFE magazine, for this is prairie pothole
country where migrating flocks of ducks and geese
pile up in numbers that Wisconsin hunters would love
to experience. But no duck hunting this trip, even if
it were fall. As we check into the motel, just another
nondescript roadside inn, I am thinking about home
and have no inkling of the bizarre experience I will
soon have.

FRIDAY 5:40 P.M.

Young adults and couples are beginning to make up a greater
portion of the crowd and sunburned parents with sleeping children in their arms are making their way towards the parking lots.
Our evening crew has clocked in, some to yet another warning
about the importance of punctuality, and our morning kids are
gone. With the shift change completed, Toni and I are reminiscing
about our years at the Fair. We enjoy doing that and being here
sparks all sorts of memories. She brings up Virginia and the years
when she helped us out at the Fair. I had forgotten about that period but the mere mention of her name brings back an avalanche
of recollections...

1950s

Virginia is grandma's niece. She and her family live in Indianapolis and are the only other Italian branch of our family that we have any relationship with. The Indianapolis connection - now that was a real Italian family. Grandma's sister Nunziatta is the matriarch there just as grandma is here in Milwaukee. Although we didn't see them often, I have vivid memories of the occasional visits. One summer my sister and I, as young kids, spent a week or two with them. The Indianapolis summer seemed much hotter than Milwaukee and I enjoyed grabbing a Coke from the freezer compartment above their fridge. These were the little glass bottles and they would come out of the freezer slightly frozen, just enough that they had a little bit of slush that truly refreshed a kid on a sultry Indianapolis summer night. I tried to replicate it at home but my Cokes always froze solid, sometimes breaking the bottle to my, and especially mom's, dismay.

We stayed in the home of Virginia's brother, Pete and his wife Katie. Pete seemed like a very intimidating guy, at least to a little kid like me. In old pictures of him, in his unbuttoned sports shirt, he seems to glare at the camera with his well-receded hair slicked back, just daring you to give him lip. In reality, he was a real teddy bear but his ice-cold glare is what stuck with me. Their son, JoJo, which I guess was a nickname for Joseph, was a little older than my sister and me and he taught us things that, if mom and dad knew, would probably result in an early ticket home. He seemed to get in trouble a lot. On one warm afternoon, we were all sitting on their front porch and JoJo pointed his unloaded BB gun at the head of his little brother. Firing it from just a foot away, something broke and a spring-loaded tubular mechanism shot out of the barrel and hit his brother smack-dab in the middle of his forehead. There was quite a bit of blood, some tears, and a whole lot of

167

yelling, but no serious injury. I hoped that mom wouldn't hear about it. I'd been negotiating for a BB gun for a long time and couldn't afford a setback; she didn't and I eventually did get the gun.

The Indy relatives had a heart-breakingly beautiful daughter, a brunette named Frances who they called Francie. When she was a teenager, she came to Milwaukee for about two weeks...actually, it was twelve and a half wonderful days...and stayed with grandma and grandpa in their small living quarters above Mille's Bar-B-Q; she helped out in the family's dairy store (a sort of deli) attached to the restaurant. This was before they converted it to a bar and cocktail lounge. One slow Sunday afternoon, I was just hanging around (she being there and all). Francie was behind the refrigerated display case, leaning casually on it and looking at me with her head propped on her hand, all lazy-like. She had the most-alluring, pixie-ish smile that accented her very high cheekbones. I remember her wearing a dark blue sleeveless blouse that day. It showed off her tanned, lean and supple arms that, for a girl, were unusually well toned - particularly so, for that pre-workout craze era. Her dark hair was cut just above the shoulders and a large, bright silver barrette on the right side held it in place. She was the kind of girl that would have a boy, or a young man even, taking stairs two at a time, just from thinking about her. We were alone and she, about seventeen and more than a few years older than me, smiled in a soft, come-hither, sexy way, saying "Amatore, why don't you come over here and give me a little kiss." I was young, about thirteen or so as I recall, and although Francie had recently replaced Margret Kreuger and even the dental assistant in my most private thoughts, I had absolutely no idea what was going on or what to do. I was extremely shy - "afraid of girls" in the language of the day - so I didn't hither and didn't get a kiss, or anything else, from Francie. But I sometimes wonder what her kiss would have been like. Certainly, one has to place differing values on the kisses accumulated over a lifetime, and a kiss – a first-kiss – from an older girl, an extremely attractive girl like Francie, to a young boy like me at that excitable age has to be worth a hundred kisses later in life.

Like probably everyone, I wish I could do certain things over again, career decisions, relationship things, all the big decisions that would seem to matter the most in the eventual reconciling of a person's time on earth. But, thinking of it now, I also wish I had gotten that kiss from Francie; maybe I would have grown up a little quicker and put Red Hot Mamma and the Penny Arcade behind me but, even if not, I would have at least enjoyed the moment – I'm sure of it – and avoided one small regret in my life.

Virginia helped us out at the Fair for a number of years during the mid to late 1970s and into the early 1980s. She was in her sixties then and always had her hair permed and perfectly coiffed. I never could understand how she managed to keep it that way at the Fair, what with all the smoke and ash dust that we deal with all day. I guess she just sacrificed a little more sleeping time than the rest of us. My oldest daughter Therese, who was a teenager at the time, would share a double bed with Virginia during the Fair. I guess the lack of sleep did strange things to all of us and Virginia once woke up in the middle of the night to see Therese propped straight up in bed, and, although still sound asleep, staring straight ahead with her eyes wide open. I don't know if Therese was talking in her sleep or not but, if she was, it was likely something like "sweet or sharp?" Most of us have those kinds of dreams –no, nightmares – where we're still at the stand in some sort of permanent hell or purgatory paying for our sins.

When Virginia is with us she gives us an update on the Indianapolis clan. I especially enjoy her stories about uncle Tony, grandma's brother-in law. Uncle Tony is an old Italian immigrant like my grandparents.

169

He is in the fruit and produce business, which is something that my grandfather did as well. Grandpa, though, just sold fruit from a cart on the streets of Milwaukee in a casual way (which was his way) many, many years ago. Uncle Tony, on the other hand, helps run the family's fruit and produce store as a full-time business. One of the classic "Uncle Tony stories" that Virginia shared happened in their market when a woman shopper decided to investigate their peaches. The Indy relatives always kept Uncle Tony away from the checkout counter and tried to keep him distant from the customers in general. Being from the old country, he didn't really get that "the-customer-is-always-right" thing and his hot Italian temper couldn't be trusted. On the day of the incident, Uncle Tony and Virginia had stacked a display of beautiful, tree-ripened peaches, the kind that you can only find now, if you're lucky, at roadside stands. They were all rosy and fuzzy and some of them even had a leaf or two still attached to the stem. I imagine, being a peach lover myself, when you smelled them they tickled your nose and filled your head with the essence of fresh peaches; I know for certain they were very juicy…and soft. As Uncle Tony swept the floor, he noticed a woman approaching the peach display. She, through squinting eyes, looked over the tempting peaches, reached out with her right hand and, with her thumb and index finger, squeezed one of the peaches (slightly, but a squeeze nonetheless). Apparently not satisfied with the results of her ripeness test, she withdrew her hand, then reached again, squeezing another of the vulnerable, ripe peaches…then another…and another. Uncle Tony stopped his sweeping and stood there, glaring at the woman. After what seemed like minutes of this, the peach abuser decided that not a single one of the Freestones was to her liking and turned away. As she walked towards the door, Uncle Tony exploded. In a decidedly-Southern Italian display of emotion he shouted out to her while, quite independently, his arms and hands went rapidly through several vernacular expressions of their own ...

"EEHHH - PUTTANA ... UNA SCHIFOSA! ...
VAFFANCULO! ... VAI IN CULO!"
Then,
"COME-A BACK, YOU MISSED-A TWO!"

Unwisely stopping in her tracks and turning back to see "which-a two" she had missed, the woman saw a red-faced Uncle Tony standing, facing her. His short Italian arms, bare from the elbow down, were tight at his sides with his hands on either side of his belt buckle. Both index fingers, right and left, were extended and pointing directly at his groin. Just in case she didn't get his drift, he flicked those pointing, chubby index fingers back and forth at his "coglioni".

The woman abruptly turned and made a hasty retreat, straight out the door. She did not "come-a back"... ever. I imagine, from that day on, she shopped for fruit and produce at the local A&P where the peaches were hard and the staff less passionate about their products.

Besides keeping us current on Uncle Tony and the Indy clan, Virginia also helps me to know my grandfather in his younger years, before I was around or old enough to remember. Grandpa was a real pisser and Virginia and her friends saw him at his best, and his worst. She told me a story from many years ago (it must have been in the 1940s) when she, a pretty young woman (I've seen photos of her), had been primping for a Saturday night dance while staying with my grandparents at the old family cottage on Wind Lake. Virginia was just as attentive to her hair then as now, probably more so, and, unbeknownst to her, as she tended to her curls and overall beautification, grandpa, who had been fishing off the little wooden pier, got an idea - a very nasty idea. I can just imagine him (he was then a handsome man of about fifty years of age) laying that old cane pole of his against the

171

low, big branch of the bigger willow tree and setting his Maxwell House Coffee can of garden worms under its shade. Propping a ladder against the edge of the cottage roof, he carried a galvanized steel bucket up the ladder and placed it on the low-pitched roof. Grandpa was still up on that cottage roof much later - only God knows how he passed the time (could he have carried a glass of his dego red up there with him?) - when she stepped out the door of the cottage, light on her feet and eager for the dance. Her hair was perfectly coiffed and she wore her best summer dress, the one the young men all liked. Then, as she swung open the screen door and stepped out...WHOOOOSH!... she was deluged by water - cold, wet, lake water, with little bits of green stuff in it. Looking up through hanging strands of soaked, black hair, there sat grandpa with his own full head of dense, silver hair and a big smile on his square-jawed face. She wound up being late to the dance and I'm certain she didn't laugh then, but she did smile in the telling of it all these years later.

Hearing Virginia's stories about Uncle Tony, and grandpa in his youth, as well as personally witnessing my grandparents' lives, makes me miss the unpolished and straightforward manner in which these old Italian immigrants lived, without pretense and with an appreciation for the juicier, dark meat of life. In today's world of political correctness and shrink-wrapped everything, I believe we've lost a lot and I'm not sure that what we've gained has really offset that loss. As for me, I'd rather see Uncle Tony passionately protecting his prized peaches than deal with some indifferent, but polite grocery clerk who doesn't really care about his peaches or even know where they came from. Somehow, watching my own grandfather eat his sheep's head, eyeballs and all, is a whole lot more interesting than seeing yet another dinner menu featuring boneless breast of chicken, and I'd be willing to bet that it probably tastes far better as well. But I'm probably not going to find any takers on that wager.

10

SHOWERS WITH
POSSIBLE CLEARING

SECOND WEEKEND: SATURDAY 8:20 A.M.

RAIN. OUR WORST FEAR IS MOCKING US WITH A COLD SPITTLE on the windshield as we drive in on Saturday morning, the second weekend and only one day from the finale. Sales have been good and we're within reach of last year's figures but now it's all up in the air...the wet, chilling air. Nothing is more cursed by us and all others like us than an all-day rain on a Saturday or Sunday. The crowd will be down to such a degree that you can't even use that word, not really. Not even bringing up the old stories of grandma and grandpa and trout fishing with special bait can get more than a slight chuckle. Not today. The cold rain soddens our prospects and spirits.

The sausage truck is waiting for us when we pull in behind the stand. It's loaded with a full, last weekend-sized delivery of Mille's Italian sausage. As handcart after handcart is wheeled into the walk-in by the Klement's deliveryman, we go through our set-up and I get the coffee going. In an act of positive thinking, I failed to pack a rain jacket this year so I buy a bright yellow plastic poncho from a concessionaire; maybe it's a good day for him, maybe not.

The fire helps. Waves of heat that were oppressive yesterday are welcome today. Flames slowly climb the wall of fresh charcoal and dampness is chased from the stand. Glowing coals attract the few who have shunned the weather. They come to the grill and hold their palms to it, like savages praying to and encouraging the rising sun.

Sales are slow. We're getting more than our share of business, thanks to the fire and its power of attraction but, in an overall sense, it's a bad day. There are days, hot days, when a brief afternoon rain, even an all-out thunderstorm, is a welcome relief from the heat and the routine. Those days, the rain just cools people off, maybe even gives them a little edge to their appetite. On a hot day like that we don't mind the rain. Back in the sixties, with women's lib and bra burning and all, it even gave us guys something to look forward to. We'd debate the transparency, the "merits" as it were, of various colored T-shirts and blouses after a good shower. Yellow and white were front-runners. White always won but, back then, we once saw a woman who, all by herself, presented a good case for yellow. The sixties were good years. Now, we're all married and not supposed to pay attention to such things…but the days are long and we've been conditioned for many years.

The rain reminds me that whenever any of us - Toni, Mark, Mike or I - would start to make claims about it looking like a good year, mom would always temper things. "Don't count your chickens …" That sort of thing. She had grown up during the depression and, for her family, like lots of families, it was a tough time - a very tough time. She never forgot those years, never took financial security for granted. In the end, she was probably right and today is making her look more right than we ever gave her credit for. Being slow, it's a good day to visit with family over at the big stand, so I do. I catch-up with Mike and Mark; Mary too. I tap beers for a while and tell Mike he's keeping a messy till, not neat like Toni and I keep ours over at the small stand. Our bills are all stacked face-up in the same direction. He doesn't care and he tells Roy to...

"Put a spit in front, Roy."

Roy complies saying with a smile, "You sound like your dad."

Mike returns the smile and adds, "Gotta have some flash."

It's still raining and I'm trying to work out how I'm going to pull one off on Mike. He's taken a liking to getting a quickie massage during his break. Some Asian fellows have a set-up where, for a few bucks they give you a neck and shoulders work-out while you sit, leaning forward with your face down in a padded rest. The next time he goes there I want to follow him and take Mary along. Once he's gotten settled in and is being rubbed-down, I want to have Mary secretly take the place of the masseur. Mike won't know of the substitution since, like I said, he'll be face down. I've told her, if we can pull it off, she can gradually start to roam a little with her hands, a little rub here, a gentle stroking down there - she knows all the right places, at least...his places. It's his reaction that I want to see - but, if he doesn't react...well, then there'll be some real explaining to do. So I just hang around and wait and say things like "It would be a good day to get a massage." Patience.

1982

It's a cold November wind that is blowing but I pay no attention to it though I'm dressed in a suit and wear no overcoat. The chill and other reminders of late autumn and even winter – dead, blowing leaves, brown grass, and a sun low to the horizon – all seem somehow fitting. It would be wrong, somehow inappropriate, today, to bother with a coat or to shy from the cold northern wind. I'm here, in Milwaukee, for the second time in just a few days which is unusual living in Michigan as I do. The year is 1982 and, other than a couple of days ago, I hadn't been here since August, for the last Fair.

Then, I had a chance late one afternoon to take her for a short walk. She was feeling well enough that day, had decided to come to the fairgrounds for a little while. I placed my arm in the crook of hers and slowly, very slowly, we walked and talked and made our way up Second Street, just as we did way back in 1959 when we tried to stop the bold relocation plans of grandpa and the cowboy. But we're relaxed now, no hurry today, couldn't go fast even if we wanted to, which we don't. Close to her, like this, I smell her unmistakable musky fragrance; it's not from a bottle nor is it unpleasant, it's just her natural scent, the one I was imprinted with as a child…as a baby more likely. I'm vaguely aware that people are looking at us, me the young man in the Mille's T-shirt (I was only in my late 30's then…young is a relative term) and "the grandma from Mille's", who's also wearing one of our T-shirts, although largely for old-times' sake. From the corner of my left eye, I see that a woman has stopped and is pointing at us, whispering to her friend. She is smiling and is obviously touched by the scene. As for me, I'm simply soaking up the quiet pleasure of the moment, realizing that there are likely few more such walks in our future ("few", I will learn, is a relative term, too). After a long, slow shuffle, we arrive at the site of The Lutheran Dining Hall where we've eaten countless meals together; the whole family has for that matter. She knows something is different and I explain that the Lutherans no longer have their place here. It's now a Polish operation but the food is good - hearty and honest food not unlike the foods that she was raised on and made a business out of. We sit down on a long bench; I tell her "fatti chiù cà" more for the teasing than for the necessity and she smiles and obliges, sliding over an inch or so. Grandma is 91 years old but her mind is still fairly sharp so we talk a little about nothing in particular. There's a soothing quality to this, not unlike the many hours spent with my head on her lap so many years before. Grandma is relaxed and at ease, as she's been for a long time, having handed the reins of the business over to dad long ago. For some time now, she has been able to sit patiently while doing absolutely nothing, a calm, peacefulness to her. On long car trips she reminds me of the Norman Rockwell painting, THE OUTING - the "before and after" two scene vacation painting; in the first scene, a family is crammed into the family car, driving to the vacation site and everyone, with one exception, looks excited and upbeat. Even the dog looks like he can't wait to jump in the lake. The second scene, post-vacation, then portrays that same family on the return drive, worn out, impatient, tired and bored, right down to the dog with lolling tongue. The grandmother, on the other hand, retains her constant equilibrium, with a stoic expression, just as in the ride up. No change; highs and lows all balanced out like she was in some deep meditation. Grandma could have posed for Rockwell's painting... had he wanted a subtle serenity to the woman's facial expression. After our few minutes of lunch together (she ate sparingly and I finished off her pork chop) we retrace our slow walk back to the stand. She will soon be driven to her home in the apartment building she owns, ever the landlord, and where she lives, alone. In a couple of days, the Fair will wrap up, I will say my farewells, and head back to my home of several years in Michigan.

Three months later in November, after the Fair and on short notice, I fly to Milwaukee on a business trip. My busy life tempts me to just fly in, attend my meeting, and fly back to Michigan. Too much going on to try to fit in a family visit. I saw everyone just a few months ago anyway. So that's what I do, but my meeting wraps up early and I have some time on my hands and sense a nagging impulse to see grandma for a few minutes before it's time to get to my return flight.

Those vague nagging feelings often have something very specific behind their persistence. In this case, I'm fairly sure it's grandpa, or, more accurately, how things went with him. As he and grandma got older, their arranged marriage, never a blissful relationship to begin with, had evolved into a difficult situation. "Arranged" had turned into disarray. Dad, at the cost of great emotional stress to himself, had to intervene and separate them, which led to what, in looking back at it now, seemed to effectively remove my grandfather from my life. He had become an angry man and that, in itself, further isolated him from me as well as from the rest of the family. He soon entered a phase of declining health, due mainly to a lifetime habit of unfiltered Camels, two packs a day, which culminated in emphysema and a cycle of nursing care, rest homes, and hospitals. Old age certainly played its inevitable part as well. One day in 1976 I got a call from dad who was out of town (I was still living in Milwaukee) telling me that grandpa had passed away in the hospital. He asked that I go there to sign the necessary paperwork. Upon entering the hospital room with the nurse I saw my grandfather's body lying on the bed, mouth agape, his head still covered with that full, dense mass of hair, now all the gray tones reduced to a final, flat white, with all color gone. After too few moments of private reflection I tended to my responsibility of the moment and was strong, which my misdirected machismo thought was now needed. Only later did I begin to regret the blocking of my feelings and, even more, not having stayed closer to him in his last years. Maybe I could have helped him keep his spirits up by talking about things that he enjoyed – certainly, anything having to do with the old country. He had always been around and willing to help me, whether it was a few bucks to buy a bullwhip or sage advice on the merits of Italian boxers, Italian opera stars and Italian kings versus those of all other nations. Grandpa's situation is something that I regret – but learned an important lesson from. How easy it must be, for someone who is aging and under duress, to fall into a pattern of negative thought...to such a degree that it affects their entire life and the relationships they value most. My grandfather had always been a light-hearted, carefree spirit, someone who was a joy to be around. If someone like grandpa could fall into such a negative pattern, how vulnerable, under similar circumstances, must the rest of us be? Knowing this, I will try to be mindful of it as I, myself, age. As for my memories of grandpa, there's an old saying that your thoughts create your reality. I believe this to be true and I prefer the reality of my grandfather as I knew him for most of my life, and that's how I will always think of...and remember him. And in that remembering, I have no regrets at all.

Now, its six years since grandpa's passing and, with my business meeting having ended early, I call dad to let him know I'm in town and have some time to stop by grandma's apartment; she hasn't been feeling well, he tells me. Nothing serious but she's really slowed down. When I arrive, grandma is sitting at her kitchen table; dad is already there since his restaurant is just across the alleyway from the apartment. Although she has no life threatening conditions, she has gone completely silent and just sits there with no apparent awareness of the world around her. I am shocked by her extreme shift of conscious-

ness and, taking her hand, I tell her, jokingly, to "fatti chiù cà" but she doesn't react except to squeeze my hand tightly when I place it in hers. She clearly is aware of my presence but is otherwise focused in another place and time. Is she reliving parts of her life? Is she, at some other level of consciousness, making plans for her future – perhaps in the presence of those who have gone before her? I don't know but I do know that she's not here at this table, at least not most of her. I say some things to her but she doesn't respond, except for that squeezing of my hand which hasn't stopped. After about a half hour of just sitting with her, hands entwined, I have to say goodbye. Since she's not physically ill, I fully expect to see her again when she's feeling better. I arrive home in Michigan a bit after dinner, just ahead of a major storm. We all go to bed at our usual times as winds rattle windows and tree limbs begin to crack and fall. Then, in the middle of the night, we are all awakened by a loud banging on our front door. I had just been dreaming of grandma, which I seldom do...was still in the dream when awakened, and her musky scent fills my head even as I shake myself awake. This dream-power seems remarkable to me and, after mentally noting it, I quickly put the thought aside. As I look through the rain spattered bedroom window, red flashing lights are visible in my driveway. Startled, I walk quickly down to the front door and, opening it, am faced by a yellow-slickered police officer. With an apprehensive tone, he tells me that the phone lines have been down in our neighborhood for some time. He goes on to tell me my father in Milwaukee, after failing to get through to me, called the local police department to ask them to get word to me. There's been a death in the family.

The funeral party has now moved into the mausoleum and the cold November wind ceases its mood-heightening effect. After a while, we all say our private farewells to grandma. None of us expected this. Mom and dad tell me that, although there is no other evidence of it, she had

*waited to see her favorite grandchild before moving on. I like to think
that's the way it really was. We all leave and rejoin each other for lunch
at Alioto's, a restaurant that caters to these situations. There, we retell
the old stories of parking fairgoer's cars and a dozen sandwiches in a
bag to go...and many more. Getting into the crowded car, afterwards,
someone tells me to "fatti chiù cà" and I smile and slide over.*

SATURDAY 11:05 A.M.

I've given up on getting Mike over to the massage place and
am back at the small stand...but why am I squinting? The permanent vertical crease in my forehead betrays my sensitivity to
sunlight and, as I look around the cash register for my sunglasses,
even though there is no sun, I realize that the cloud cover, which
has brought us this all-day rain, must be dispersing. Could it be?
Looking to the still-gray sky above, I see no breaks in the clouds
but there's been a definite change, subtle, yes, but definitely a
change. Noon is still an hour away and if the weather breaks we
can still salvage the day...do very well even. Twenty minutes later, I
check the skies again and there, off to the north, about in line with
the Giant Slide, is a very small patch of blue. Now I've got Mark
on the phone over at the other place and he and the whole crew
there are upbeat. They've noticed the sudden change as well and
we both check our fridges and start to think about getting some
more sausages put on the spits - it's going to be a big day. Mom
just worries too much.

Mom selling 10 cent sandwiches
at Milwaukee lakefront – 1936

Grandma's favorite – 1940s

1979

It's hot in Swift Current, Saskatchewan in late July and Chuck cranks up the old window-mounted air conditioner in our small double room...two twin beds about five feet apart. I throw my duffle on the bed nearest the door, he takes the other. Funny, just a few months on the road together and we already have our routines down. I always take the door-side bed. Not wanting to unhook the sausage wagon from the truck, nor deal with trying to find a big-enough parking spot, we ask the desk clerk about a place to eat within walking distance. The elderly fellow in a dirty, International Harvester cap that looks like it might have once been red suggests the truck stop adjacent to the motel, so we make it easy on ourselves. My meal disappoints. I've got a couple of pork chops on my plate but they're "flaked and formed" according to the (overlooked) fine print on the menu - which I guess means that scraps of meat are ground up and pressed into a pork chop shaped mold. Not good; makes me yearn for the big pork chops (NOT flaked and already possessed of their own, nature-provided form) of the Wisconsin State Fair. It will begin in just a few days but we have a gig in New York City, a street festival. Funny, that's how grandma and grandpa started this whole sausage business of ours, at religious street festivals in Milwaukee; the expression "full circle" comes to mind. That was even before their first appearance, with dad's help, at the State Fair in 1932. Dad was only sixteen that first year. All things considered, I'd rather be in Wisconsin than trying to avoid low overhead bridges in New York.

We've been sleeping now for what must be several hours. I'm lying in my twin bed on my right side and I realize that I've just found myself in a trance-like half-awake, half-asleep state and that I've apparently had my eyes open for a while. I can faintly see Chuck's form in his bed just a few feet from me and I can hear his soft snoring. Laying there, with my eyes open, I then hear my name spoken, my nickname of Matt, not Amatore. The voice is soft and that of a female and it's coming from a few feet behind me:

"Matt...." the voice beckons, soft but clear. Hearing it, I am startled and spooked - freaked out, to be frank. I know that there is no person in the room other than Chuck and myself. The door was locked and latched and the voice has an ethereal quality to it; the voice is clear and it is real but it is not from any living person in this room. Too spooked to turn and look, I just lay there, seeing my roommate's back five feet away and I continue to hear his snore... and then the voice repeats itself:

"Matt...", again, in a soft, beckoning tone.

I have had some strange experiences in my life, but nothing as bizarre as this. I remain, frozen in place, with my eyes wide open for several minutes - the voice is now silent; twice it spoke, then it was gone. With the voice silent, I gradually build up the courage to turn over in bed and, as expected, the room is empty with nothing at all unusual or out of place. The door to the room remains closed, locked, and latched. In the morning, I thought about the voice, tried to reason it out, but it defied all explanation, all logic- based rationalization. I would wonder about this experience for many years to come, even now, and can only assume that it came from some source, perhaps even a subconscious part of me, that needed to be heard. By the end of the day I decided to fly back to my home in Michigan for a couple of days. I arrived unannounced and unexpected and saw my wife and three children - Therese, Jennifer, and Matthew - in the front yard of our home as my cab pulled into the driveway. It was wonderful to be home with my family and they were thrilled to see their dad, and husband, after a long summer without him. We all enjoyed a few summer days together and then I was off again - not to the New York street festival (where my brother-in-law, Joe, would help Chuck during my absence) but to Wisconsin to join the family there for the Wisconsin State Fair.

It had become clear to me. The siren song of the international fair and exposition circuit disguised a life-style that was not for me, not alone, not like this. Dad's comment about "sawdust in your veins" now had a harsh reality to it. Mostly though, while I loved the adventure of traveling to places like Tucson and Calgary where my western yearnings were teased, I had come to realize, up there on a slope of the Canadian Rockies, that my attraction to the fair circuit was naïve. It had been driven by my experience of being with my family at The Wisconsin State Fair for all of my life. Without dad and mom, grandma and grandpa, without Toni, Mike and Mark, the real appeal of the Fair - any fair - was missing. The children were a big part of it too, being with them as they began to help out in the stand, learning the ropes, or running back, all excited from some adventure in the fairgrounds. The North American circuit with its barkers and colored balloons were all just flash; they had a certain attraction, but the real substance was in being with family. My real yearnings were there, not to a life on the road away from everyone. This was a difficult and expensive lesson but an important one, at least it was for me. I would, after this year's State Fair, salvage our season by completing our tour out East and then dad and I would sit down and work out a plan. We would sell the truck and he would use the sausage wagon at other local Milwaukee venues, and do so quite profitably. I would, after this season, go back to my career in information technology sales, where I would push that big rock up the hill, year after year, just like Sisyphus again, but at least be able to look forward to putting that behind me for eleven days in August ...every August.

It was around this time that I received an unusual and revealing document from dad. I think he had been cleaning out his dresser drawers, where he kept a few important papers. It had a handwritten note stapled to the front of it - one of those pre-printed forms with a humorous statement. This one, on yellow paper, was headed: "Once You're Over The Hill ...You Pick

Up Speed." On that cover sheet, in dad's chicken-
scratch handwriting was the note: "To your question:
What did you do in the war daddy? - This is what I
did and why I was too important to be sent overseas
– (signed) Dad" His comment, light-heartedly joking
though it was, also revealed a significant heart-felt
truth, as joking comments often do. The attachment
was a copy of his military discharge papers. It docu-
mented a discharge date of October 28, 1945. More
importantly, it detailed an educational background
and service record steeped in science. A degree from
Marquette University and post-grad studies at The
University of Wisconsin, assignments as a chemist
and bacteriologist, and a later position in New Mexico
where, according to the document, he "ran chemical
determinations in connection with high altitude an-
oxia to determine cause and remedy of physiological
effects due to high-altitude flying." Dad's background
in the service was not completely unknown to me and
my siblings. We had all heard dad mention working
with pilots and high altitude chambers before, always
with a sense of pride, but never at any level of detail.
We had also seen old photos of him in the desert landscape of New Mexico. But now I had an understand-
ing of the extent of dad's advanced education and early
career in science; the old, vintage Bausch and Lomb
microscope that we found in our basement suddenly
had new meaning and, just as with those old, blurry
glass slides, it clarified my dad's life for me. Here was a
man who had put away his microscope and put aside a

promising career in order to become an entrepreneur, much like his mother. She, I subsequently learned, had wanted him to pursue a medical degree, which he certainly was well on his way toward accomplishing. But, in the end, his own dream of self-employment won out and the Italian sausage business at the Fair became a top priority for both him and grandma. In the end, the immigrant woman and her son were more alike then either of them ever realized. Now, all these years later, it's clear that in the pursuit of his own dream dad created something more significant then he, or grandma, could have anticipated - here's my old friend serendipity calling on me again - he created an annual tradition that has kept our far-flung family together and given us a place and time to rejoin each other and, in our own way, honor our heritage.

SATURDAY 1:40 P.M.

"Most of the parking lots are full" a woman customer pushing a young girl in a stroller tells me, "I had to drive all around before I found a place to park." That statement is like a shot in the arm. The sun has been out for about an hour now. The puddles are drying up, and the park is now getting crowded. It's just early afternoon and we have the best part of Saturday ahead of us.

Les is cooking here at the small stand and over the last couple of days we've been talking about our mutual interest in military history. He ambles over to me at the register while keeping an eye on the grill. His father, he tells me, had been in some of the most intense action of the Korean "conflict" - which seems a real euphemism, especially for the families of those many soldiers who died over there. At a reservoir called Chosin in the dead of the 1950 winter, Les's dad was among a force of 20,000 that were surprised and surrounded when 200,000 Chinese volunteers poured across the border into North Korea. They fought a valiant but losing effort. When asked if he was retreating, a Major General by the name of Smith was reported as saying, "Retreat, hell! We're attacking in a different direction!" Some say he was misquoted but I like to think he really said it.

Our conversation evolves in reverse chronology as we touch on the Civil War and the American Revolutionary War. The sausages are getting a little too brown and I have to remind Les, and myself, to pay attention to the fire. With that under control, I tell Les about some interesting old military artifacts, (my wife calls it all junk) I've found over the years. I mention this to Les in a casual conversation; no big deal. He seems interested but I misinterpret and will, much later, pay the price for letting down my guard.

I'm at the grill now, spelling Les for a few minutes while he has a half hour break. He's left me with good, hot, coals and, because business has been steady, cooking will be easy. After removing a spit of cooked and ready sausage, I put another raw spit on the grill; have to keep up the pace. Looking out at the mid-afternoon crowd walking past I notice a guy carrying a huge stuffed animal. It looks like an elephant and it's not much smaller than the real thing. This one's purple but I've seen them in other colors as well. Every time I see one of these things ("plush" is what the carnies call them) being schlepped around the park I can't help but recall my brother Mike's many trips to the carnival games as a little kid.

Most of the game operators recognized him as a budding sharpie[20] and cringed whenever he walked up to their joint, even stopping their grind, hoping he'd pass on by to some other game. What some of them didn't know, however, was that the eight year old kid's family was well-connected with the State Fair Police, heck, the entire police force of West Allis, Wisconsin for that matter. For years, the local cops had all known grandma, grandpa, and dad from Mille's Bar-B-Q, just across Greenfield Avenue from the fairgrounds, where they would stop by just to visit and chat. And, of course, they'd visit with them during the Fairs, going all the way back to 1932. Well, one day - this would have been around 1956 when he was eight - little Mike walked up to a flat store in the midway and paid his money to play. The operator, an alibi agent, who was new, took him for a mark and was surprised when the kid copped a nice prize, a long handled chrome flashlight, by flipping a hoop over the flashlight and around the very tight fitting wooden block it stood on. The agent, of course, told Mike that he hadn't really won the prize, giving him excuse after excuse. My little brother stormed off and found dad. Within minutes the two of them, along with the State Fair Chief of Police were back at the flat joint. The excuses stopped, a severe warning was issued and Mike walked away with the bright, shiny flashlight, to the envy of both Mark and me.

As Mike grew older, he became the scourge of the midway. By the time he hit high school he was copping two gigantic stuffed

---

20 Carnie-speak : Sharpie - someone who is very good at beating the skill games and winning expensive prizes; Joint or Store - a skill game; Grind - the pitch being yelled by the operator or agent; Flat Store - a game that brings in a lot of cash by offering expensive prizes which are seldom won; Mark - a typical target, a person who will play and lose; Alibi Agent - an operator of a flat store who makes excuses as to why the player didn't win ("cop") a prize.

animals every day he felt like playing; the limit was normally two prizes a day and he always maxed out. Elephants, giraffes, birds, fish, dinosaurs, teddy bears, tigers, lions, dogs, gorillas - I'm talking over one hundred; he personally filled the bedrooms of every girl he ever dated, but one in particular, Mary, who would become his wife, got the most and the best. Her room looked like a carnival version of Noah's ark right down to the two-by-two, and the overflow made its way into the rooms of her three sisters. How could the poor girl not fall in love with him?[21]

How did he do it? All these years later, he finally told me his secret to his favorite skill game. This was the one where you pitch dimes at a bunch of glass plates that are stacked at various levels. It looks easy, but it isn't. It's a flat store where you have very little chance of winning. Back then, the plates were waxed, probably still are, and the dimes just bounce off or slide off. What little Mike did (still could, I'm sure) was to first warm up the dime by rubbing it with his fingers. Then he'd look for a plate that happened to have a slight slant or tip to it, where the higher end was furthest away from him - that was key. With his target selected, he'd flip the dime in "heads or tails" fashion at the back end of the plate. When he did it just right and the dime's flipping rotation was just so (there's still some luck involved) the dime would bounce forward and stay on the plate. Bingo! "I'll take that big orange orangutan over there. Can you give me some more dimes for this dollar? Thanks."

Now, I don't mean to imply that it's all in knowing the trick; skill is important and Mike was always the champion of the family in any game or sport that required finesse. As kids, he would regularly fleece me of my spare change when we played penny

---

21   And, to this day, he also remains very popular with Mary's three sisters, Beth, Ann, and Margaret.

toss at home, where the object was to make your penny land as close as possible to a line on the floor without crossing over it. In high school, while I did well in football and track where speed and strength were important, he focused on tennis and golf. Now, all these years later, he can easily beat me at those sports and we seldom have opportunities to compete in the long jump or play tackle football.

SATURDAY 10:50 P.M.

Fireworks are exploding and we're in the last hours of what's turned out to be a very good day. We've just run out of peppers and have to serve the sandwiches without them; but that's still not an excuse for putting ketchup or mustard on a Mille's. Brian just came over here to the small stand; he's got a cold Spotted Cow from the microbrew tent for me and he's sipping on one himself. Nice guy, that Brian. I guess now that he's tying his apron in the back he feels he has plenty of slack to work with and I'm actually glad to see he's enjoying State Fair food and drink again since it all wraps up tomorrow, on Sunday. He tells me there's another scam going on over at the big stand, and he's in on it. Seems that one of the guys came up with the idea of sabotaging Roy's chocolate éclairs tonight. Roy buys a couple of éclairs from Starlite every night and takes them home for his next morning's breakfast. Yummy! Well, the pranksters (can Les be far away?) sucked the fresh custard out of Roy's éclairs and inserted…you guessed it…a cooked Italian sausage into each of the resulting cavities. France meets Italy. Now, lest the reader jump to poor Roy's defense, I would suggest that there are probably several tasty treats, popular with many of us, that were developed under similar, unintended circumstances…I just can't think of any right now but I'm almost certain they exist. Serendipity happens. Also, Brian is, himself, a perpetrator, so it's also a case of peer persecution, and we Mille boys are merely interested observers. My thirteen-year old stepson Tyler would later tell me that Les and Brian tried to recruit him to do the sucking part but he refused.

I ask Brian if he's put on some weight (he thinks so) and congratulate him on the éclair prank they've set-up. We then toast Spotted Cows to its success.

11

JET LAG

ELEVENTH DAY; SUNDAY 8:25 A.M.

SUNDAY MORNING, LAST DAY OF THE FAIR AND THE FEELING IS strange and contentious. A part of me is looking forward to getting back to my home in Philly, being with my wife Margaret and little kids, Jack and Juliette, who I've greatly missed, and getting a good night's sleep. But there's also a true melancholy that permeates my mind. Although we've had fun, the work has been hard and the days long. But its been such a familiar, comfortable routine and the reconnection with Toni, Mike, Mark and the others has only begun to fill a yearning that is difficult to describe or explain, but it's there nonetheless. Toni is staying on another day and will be going out to dinner with the rest of the family. Although I don't mention it, I would really enjoy being able to join them - but I can't, not enough vacation days. Tyler and I will arrive in Philly late tonight and I'll be up at 5:15am tomorrow morning to head up to

Manhattan. So, we pack our bags and take them along in our drive to the fairgrounds. I also bring along the big, green, soft-sided cooler bag that I will load with blue ice and twenty pounds of fresh sausage before we leave for home. Neighbors and friends, the close ones, are all awaiting their annual taste of Mille's Italian Sausage.

We've just picked up Roy on the ride to the park and, cramming into the rear seat next to me, he looks as tired as the rest of us. Maybe even more so, since he, Les, Mikey, Brian, and Nick, their designated driver, went out to Mama Mia's, a restaurant/bar on 78th and Burleigh, for beers after we closed up last night. After a reasonable waiting period, Mike asks, smiling...

"So Roy, how were your éclairs this morning?"

"I don't know, I didn't get to eat 'em," he hoarsely replies, enviously eyeing my travel cup of coffee. He knows it's a good, strong, Italian roast, freshly brewed at The Java House in Cedarburg.

"What do you mean?"

"My roommate got in late last night, really drunk. He saw 'em in the 'fridge and ate 'em both" Roy casually says, rubbing the sleep from his eyes, never even smiling.

"What?... did he say anything?"

"Not really; just scarfed 'em down... he liked 'em, that's for sure." After a good laugh from the rest of us, Tyler tells Roy what his buddies did to the pastries, with an emphasis on the sucking-the-custard-out-of-the-éclair part and Roy, now rubbing his stubble, joins in...amused at both the prank itself as well as its foiled outcome. I then say something about how good my coffee tastes, adding "nice and strong" and watch as Roy's eyes, bags and all, slowly move to focus in on the steaming cup in my hand. Moments later Mikey mercifully hands Roy a big cup of the Italian roast that he had concealed at his feet...Roy smiles and expresses his appreciation as he quickly rips the sip-hole tab from the lid. All is well as we continue on to the fairgrounds.

Mark and Donna arrived at the big stand ahead of us this morning and are already opening up, with Brian's help. It's a beautiful morning and the dark interior of the stand is quickly filled with daylight as the side flaps, then the front flaps all go up for yet another day. The sausage deliveryman is waiting for us with the final sausage order and he, always friendly, asks how we're doing and if we've had a good Fair. As the guy who delivers our sausage every day, he probably knows the answer to that question even before he asks it. He's not wearing a hard hat, never does. I tell him he's living life on the edge without one, working without a net, so to speak…then fill him in about the delivery guy in the 1960s. Mike then reminds me what that guy's kid had said about him. They're all good stories and we never tire of hearing them but, every once in a while, one of us will remember one that has been overlooked for a few years - and so, we'll add it to our over-worked repertoire.

Such was the case with the paella story that resurfaced just the other day, poking its ugly little head back into our collective consciousness. It was at the Fair, not so many years ago; I had a craving for what had become one of my favorite dishes, paella, that great Spanish classic of rice and mixed meats and seafood. I had gotten my paella recipe version from a Williams Sonoma catalog that pooh-poohed the mixed-meats part - the Chorizo sausage, rabbit, and chicken - in favor of shrimp. I guess it was a midweek day when I rolled up my sleeves, figuratively, and launched into the project. Now, this was not a humorous incident, not at the time. In fact, I'm pretty sure I irritated the others considerably, although they mostly just ignored me until, after hours of shirking my other responsibilities, I finally presented my lovely little masterpiece for everyone to enjoy. And therein laid the rub, specifically, those two words, "little" and "everyone." Not even two pounds of shrimp can go very far when the Mille's, with extended Fair week family, have all been saving their appetites for a special meal. That day there was dad, Toni, Mike, Mark, Mary, Donna, Megan, Nick, Joe, Becky, Roy, and, of course, Brian (how could I say no those pleading eyes?) The portions were tiny - had to be - and while eating, someone, I think it was Mark, was heard to say "hey, I found a shrimp, what did I win"? Not much of story, I know, but they like to kid me about it, so I let them (as if I had a choice).

Brian, Les, Roy, and Mikey are all focused on getting their morning start-up tasks completed early so they can have a quick breakfast together at the Starlite next to the livestock barns. Les looks even rougher than Roy this morning and the four of them are laughing, painfully it seems, at comments about pitchers of beer and gin on the rocks. Les is laughing less than the others and has very little to say this morning. His eyes are so bloodshot I can't help but suggest that, were he to be charging an entrenched enemy, military-minded as he is, an adversary properly tutored to "not shoot till you see the whites of their eyes", he would arrive unscathed. But he's not amused so I just leave him alone.

Following the pepper juice trail once again, I push our last supply of peppers on the green handcart toward the small stand. Everything seems to be a little behind schedule today but that's not unusual for a last weekend Sunday. The "Guess Your Age or Weight" guy on the corner is not yet there but he tends to get a late push on Saturday nights and probably got out pretty late. As I pass by the State Fair Information Booth I can't help but imagine how well any of us, the Mille family that is, could just jump right in there and go to work. Where's the Baked Potato place? Who serves the best wings? Where can I find an ATM? How late are the buildings open? Where's the Lost and Found children place? Back when they were little kids, all of the grandchildren - mom's and dad's that is ... Mikey, Missy, Megan, Therese, Matty, and Jennifer... spent so much time running around the Fair, often with mom, that any of them, even as six year olds, could have staffed this information booth as well as any adult, maybe better. Now, some of them, and their parents, even have the answers to the more obscure questions: Who makes the best coffee? (We do, assuming Roy hasn't sabotaged it... but we don't sell it.) Best sandwich that's not made by Mille's? (The rib-eye steak at Cattlemen's Association.) Coolest, old re-discovered State Fair-related paintings? (The huge mural-sized paintings displayed in the Wisconsin Products Building.) Most interesting exhibit? (The State Fair Museum spot in the Exposition Center - but that's just me.) The best public restrooms with no waiting line? (I'm not telling!)

Now I'm at the small stand and I've wheeled the bottled water cooler to the curb out front. As I drain the water from yesterday's melted ice, I get the usual smirking glances from the few early birds walking past. This cooler, being cylindrical or barrel shaped, about three feet high and having a domed top, has a striking resemblance to STAR WARS' R2D2, at least in terms of shape and size. When I whip-out the curiously positioned six-inch drain hose and open its valve, an arc of water from the melted ice shoots out from the flaccid tube into the storm sewer drain just in front. I get giggles every day and even notice that some guys quickly look away, homophobes for certain. The women all just laugh and, if they're looking when the draining is about done, I'll give the hose a shake or two before I tuck it away. That's always good for a cheap laugh or even an admonishment to make sure I wash my hands.

Wide-bodied Schwarzenegger-looking guys (early version) in low-scooped bodybuilder shirts are muscling their way through the growing crowd. Many are joined at the hip with equally low body-fat, tanned, blond haired young women. Clearly, this is a big day for physique minded men and women - and the judging will start later in the afternoon at the International Amphitheater. I imagine most of these guys and maybe even some of the women could give that old bell, the one that used to be over near the 84th Street entrance many years ago, a good clang.

With my opening routine complete, Toni watches over things while I go out for breakfast and, hoping to get a few minutes with the boys who should be at the Starlite, I head over there. As I walk past the Giant Slide and see the Sidewalk Sundae booth nearby I think of the day years ago - *these stories are true and need to be heard; don't blame me!* - when all the stars lined up and someone finally asked The Question just the right way. I can't make any great claim to witticism, at least not the quick, on-the-spot variety; I'm the guy who usually comes up with the perfect comeback about a day and a half later, which is actually a good trait for a memoirist but has little value in social settings. No, I had actually had this little gem ready for a couple of years and, although I enjoyed Sidewalk Sundaes, those tasty slabs of vanilla ice cream served on a stick (Paddle Pop style) as much as the next guy, and bought one every few days during the Fair, I was never asked The Question in just the right way, so my one-liner had remained on the shelf.

She was cute and, fortunately, not too young (that would have created a dilemma of propriety that I would not have wanted to wrestle with.) As I walked up to the little stand on that glorious day, I didn't have The Question on my mind, perhaps having, in effect, given-up after so many failed attempts. So I just asked the girl for "one vanilla, please." Then, out of nowhere, I heard it, The Question:

"Crushed nuts?"

In the past, The Question had never been offered in just the right, simple, two-worded perfection, the only way this could ever work. But today, I got it - a high hanging curve ball, and without hesitation I smiled and answered with,

"No, I always walk this way."

She took it well, very well, and I'm pretty sure she gave me a few extra nuts. I think she was impressed by my quick wit and I hope she doesn't read this book.

The Starlite is a popular and good breakfast spot and I arrive there to see the waitress taking the orders of the Mille cooks - Les, Roy, Brian and Mikey. Nick, last's night's designated driver is not along, him not having the same need for breakfast food as the others. I sit at the table next to them and nod with a smile in reply to their grunting acknowledgement of my presence. While considering my own choices, I hear frustration in Les's voice as he struggles to communicate with the young girl taking his order. All he wants is two eggs over-easy with bacon but either he's not asking the right way or the menu choice doesn't provide that selection. It's beginning to look like the Jack Nicholson restaurant scene in FIVE EASY PIECES and Les's hung-over condition is not conducive to patience on his part. Then, after a couple attempts at logic and special consideration fail to end his misery (self-inflicted, for sure), he throws his arms in the air and fairly screams, "Oh, For The Love OF GOD!!" ...with the emphasis on the "of God" part, then rests his beleaguered head on the table atop his folded arms in a gesture of total defeat and surrender. With that, I make a mental note to keep an eye on his cooking today.

Conversation is light as we all quickly eat our breakfasts (Les did get his bacon and eggs) and I walk the block or so back to the big stand. I want to get there with Brian since Mark told me he was going to fully disclose the apron prank to him when he got back from breakfast. Knowing Mark, his method of "full disclosure" might be worth watching. Mike and I are talking about the sausage supply. It looks like we're going to come out in good shape without a lot of excess inventory. While talking, we keep our eyes on Brian, who is about to start an hour or so of sausage spitting and has just grabbed his apron from the nail in the kitchen. Its fit comfortably since he eschewed the traditional front knotting method in favor of the far less demanding (of length) rear knot. Slipping the loop of the still pretty-clean green apron over his large neck, it hangs just above those impressive calves of his. Now, at the moment of truth, his hands reach behind his back to grab and tie the strings. A weird expression, puzzlement is how I would describe it, takes over his face, as he gropes, searching vainly for something that's not there.

"What the..." but his voice trails off and he stares, now, at the useless one inch stubs, struggling to understand what happened to his apron. Looking up in bewilderment, he catches the smirk on the faces of Mark and Mike and suddenly realizes they had something to do with this - but it takes a moment longer for the full implication of this to sink in before he feels the real impact.

"Aww, you,........" he pauses, struggling to not lose his temper while his easy-to-read face begins to flush, realizing he's been had *big-time*, then just cuts it off with "........guys" with the missing words understood by the tone of his voice and facial expression. But, within seconds, he accepts his fate and comes out of the kitchen with a red-faced smile, counter-punching all the way. We all re-hash the whole sordid affair and when he finds out that Mark was its chief architect, he cusses him out and makes a vow of vengeance - in a nice way. But, even now, a third level of awareness hits him as he connects the dots and recalls some of the State Fair snacks he thought about having but had passed on. For Brian, today will be a day of feasting, not fasting. He has some catching up to do. A new classic has been created and it will join the ranks of the best of the Mille's Italian Sausage State Fair stories. The thing is, I suspect that were he asked, Brian would admit to a sense of pride at being a key player in the apron strings prank, it being world-class and all.

2000

For Toni, it seems like any other State Fair day. It's a Wednesday, senior citizen's day in the park, and the year is 2000. Dad has slowed down a lot over the prior few months and has joined us at the Fair for just a few days this year. This is one of those days. With the small stand opened-up and ready for business, my sister asks me to watch over things while she takes a few minutes off. No problem. I notice that she is walking off towards the big stand, where I know dad is relaxing. He's with Mary, Mike and Mark - Donna too. I wonder what Toni is up to as I watch elderly men and women walk slowly past our stand, a few with walkers, most without. While she's gone, Earl Trader has stopped by to say hello as he does every year on senior's day. Earl is one of mom and dad's old gang. He, his now deceased wife, and a handful of others, were constant companions and partygoers when they were in their twenties, thirties and forties, until families and jobs slowed them down a little. Earl is an amazing specimen; always a rakishly

Mom and grandchildren – Mikey, Therese (rear), Melissa, Megan, and Matthew in 1967

Mark, Margaret, Juliette, Mike, and Amatore

Dad and the "management team" – Mike, Toni, Amatore, and Mark in 2000

handsome man, right down to his Errol Flynn-style moustache, he still looks terrific, walks miles every day and although in his late eighties, is a terror with the younger women. Big band orchestra music is coming from across the boulevard-like mall as I catch-up with Earl and we eventually say goodbye till next year.

Later and pretty much on schedule, Toni returns looking pensive but happy.

"Where'd you go?" I ask, more out of curiosity than anything, as I crack open a roll of quarters on the till drawer.

"Dad and I just had a couple of dances together over at Budweiser" she says in a lilting voice, smiling broadly now, her eyes a bit misty... "just like we used to."

With that, she proceeds to wax nostalgic and tells me about dad teaching her to dance at the Modernistic Ballroom which had stood within a hundred feet of here, many years ago. She describes how good a dancer he always was, how she would stand on his feet when very young, there at the Modernistic, and, when older, would learn and practice the Mambo and other popular dances with him. I had forgotten about the Modernistic but enjoyed dusting off the memory of it. I could imagine the two of them there, all those many years ago when he helped her and how she undoubtedly had helped him along the dance floor today; full circle...and fitting.

SUNDAY 2:55 P.M.

Brian is in a good mood and the day goes on. Toni helps me pack my twenty pounds of sausage to take back to Philadelphia. We pack them in zip-lock freezer bags, five sausages to a bag, and in my mind, I click off the names of friends and neighbors who will be favored with a gift baggie when I get to Philly. They all eagerly look forward to it each year, Dot and Otto, Brendan and Jen, the Smoldas and a few others - it's a small but special list and their appreciation more than makes up for the effort. My green thermal bag is now jam packed with baggies; it must look like some sort of drug operation about to go down and, come to think of it, the eagerness of the recipients on the other end isn't too inconsistent with that. We bag some sharp peppers too and, with the skill of a cross-country furniture mover, jam them into the only remaining space, a tiny void in one corner of the flexible green bag. With great difficulty I zip the bag shut and begin my perennial worry: what if Midwest loses the bag? Will some baggage handler in Newark or Dubuque be calling his friends tomorrow, inviting all of them over for a grill party? I worry about these things. Putting it out of my mind for the moment, Toni and I talk about getting together next month at my place to put-up some sharp peppers, the old way, for our own use.

The day has sped by. It's now late in the afternoon and think-ing about tomorrow, there's a reluctance to go back to my regular job. I'll have to hit the ground running when I land in Philly and will go through the big transition once again. It's a little like jet lag but more mental than physical and not due to time zones but, rather, environment and attitude. In a curious way, it seems that the "jet lag" effect has been more difficult to recover from when Eastbound than Westbound. Used to be, I thought this difficult transition had to do with the fun atmosphere of fairs versus the world of business suits. My experience as an itinerant Fair vendor one long summer years ago had exposed that as a thin veneer... flash which masked the real attraction. Now I know what the Mil-waukee-bound flight means to me and why I quickly forget about technology sales forecasts but easily remember how to deal with a difficult spit of sausage - even a "spinner" - or a customer who has had too many beers. Conversely, when arriving back in Philly, I seem to hang on to my State Fair-self like a man who can't let go of an old love. I look at old State Fair photos, I write emails to Les, I even look into the possibility of stabling a horse - a shiny, black Percheron for sure - at a nearby stable with the impractical idea of winter sleigh rides through Valley Forge National Park, just up the street from my home, with my kids. Stopping by to ask the Valley Forge rangers about it, they tell me it's allowed; no problem. But the stable can't accommodate me and, after a while, I'm busy with business meetings, teacher conferences, and swim meets and let the whole thing slide - for another year. But I know I'll be back in Wisconsin and I now know why I wouldn't miss it for the world.

My life has had many twists and a few turns. Marriages, children, divorce, career changes, successes and failures have all been instrumental, just as they are in the lives of most. Wisconsin, Michigan, and various parts of Pennsylvania, each has been a home to me. Information technology, a year on the North American fair circuit, and back to technology; my career has taken a number of spins. But, in the midst of all this ongoing change there has been one - and only one - true constant in my life. That has been my family and our times together at The Wisconsin State Fair, operating Mille's Italian Sausage, for a few summer days, this year and every year...as children, as teenagers, adolescents, husbands and wives, fathers and grandparents. I have come to finally appreciate my time at the Fair for what it really is and have found ease and contentment in this. In the past, I would sometimes consider the days spent here as an imposition on my valuable personal time, vacation time, and it certainly does eat into my annual allotment of two to three weeks, depending. But the trick is in realizing that these are very special days and while working hard, to take a lesson from grandpa and smell the roses too; make it a special working-vacation of sorts, for when else will I see all of my brothers and my sister again? At the Fair we see each other, we rehash the old stories and create some new ones and we each - certainly I can at least say it of myself - find a part of ourselves that we may have lost or forgotten about over the last twelve months. For about fifty weeks of each year I will live in suburbia and chase the American dream. I'll wear a suit and other nice clothes, love and enjoy my wife and children, go to soccer games and cut my lawn before it gets too long, and try to save money for retirement. But, when I get back to the State Fair, enter the Coliseum and see the Percherons and farm families I will remember a part of myself that I had forgotten but will never completely lose. TV cowboys, Indian mounds, and an old red bandanna - they all come back to the surface and for eleven days I will let them play in my mind, vicariously.

The old folks are waiting for me at the State Fair too; I only have to walk past the Polish place (still the Lutheran Dining Hall in my mind) to remember my last, slow walk with grandma and our earlier, faster walk up that same street, when the sight of a cowboy in a pick-up with our frail wooden stand in tow stopped us dead in our tracks. Should I decide to skewer some lamb chops and roast them on the grill, grandpa with his mischievous, dancing eyes and thick, bulletproof hair, all silvery and gunmetal gray, will be with me, making sure I don't burn the grated Romano cheese that makes them special. As for dad, he came to his last Fair in the year 2000. Toni and he had that final, slow dance then. She didn't know it would be their last dance, not for certain that is, but she probably suspected it. He left us all when he passed away just a few weeks later; but he is remembered by me, Toni, Mike and Mark

every day we're together at the Fair, and every time we tell Roy, or
Les, or Brian to put a spit of sausage up front, and hang it high,
for flash.

September; Philadelphia

Email messages are flying fast and furious. Most of them are quickies: plan on attending the conference in Florida next month; a reply from a company that I've been trying to meet with, notice of my employer's holiday schedule for next year, and on and on. I'm sitting at my desk in my home office outside of Philadelphia with my laptop in front of me; no commute to New York today. The Fair ended a month ago, I've completed my transition, and I'm back in the routine, doing my Sisyphus act. It's early on a Wednesday morning and I'm about through with all of the messages that have hit my inbox since yesterday, but then a new arrival suddenly pops up. This one stands out from all the earlier ones; this one snaps me out of my early morning stupor faster than my strong-brewed coffee, safe from Roy's meddling, could ever do. Suddenly forgetting all about reservations for flights to Florida and not caring which day of the week Christmas falls on anymore, I quickly click on the new arrival. It's from ILuvBrit Buttons@ Yahoo.com and the email subject line reads "Info re.Your Elephant Button".

First, a little bit of background: Over a year ago I had posted an inquiry to a British-based internet message board, a group of British military history buffs. My question concerned an interesting military button I'd found at the site of an old British fort that sat near the US-Canadian border around 1815. It's an interesting button and has the image of an elephant on the front, so it must designate a British regiment that served in India. Way back then I got a few replies from the Brits but nothing conclusive. Those replies had been on my mind for some time but then I had totally forgotten about them. So now, I have a reply that's linked to my old posting, which I'd assumed to be inactive for a long time - but there it is, my original message number, subject, and all. With my hopes for conclusive feedback soaring I eagerly click and open the message...and read it:

Hi, I saw your posting about the elephant button. Based on your description, I can tell you it is NOT associated with any British military regiment. It actually was worn by an itinerant carnival performer, or "carnie". This individual was know to perform stunts with a wheel and would travel from carnival to carnival. I hope this is helpful.

Best Wishes,
I Luv Brit Buttons

My hope quickly shifts to extreme annoyance. What kind of a button expert is this person anyway? He or she has no idea what they're talking about and I can't simply ignore this stupid response.

Actually, I could but this is more than annoying, it challenges the authenticity of one of my favorite artifacts and it's from someone who obviously deems himself, or herself, to be an expert (for no apparent reason) and that just goes right up my butt. Forgetting everything else, I quickly click the Reply icon and begin to key-in my own message:

> *Hi, Thank you for your email but your information is ABSO-LUTELY INCORRECT. I personally recovered this button from the site of a British fort that was established upon the signing of the Treaty of Ghent in 1815. I found it "in situ" at a very isolated site in association with other British military artifacts of that period, so I am certain of its authenticity. Thanks anyway.*

Shaking my head and glad to be rid of Mr. (or Miss?) Buttons, I get back to work but, minutes later, am interrupted by yet another email message. It's, again, from the button person:

> *Hi, I'm sorry to disappoint you but your button is not authentic. Too bad.*
>
> *Sorry,*
> *I Luv Brit Buttons*
> *ps – The Philadelphia Eagles Suck!*

It takes me a few seconds to get my bearings. I'm disoriented…. confused. What's with the Eagles slur? Then it hits me. I have just been victimized by the master prankster himself. I Luv Brit Buttons is, in fact, Les. The Eagles disparagement reeked of his touch. Somehow, he had found my year-old post on the internet and set-up an email identity of "I Luv Brit Buttons" and then set the trap; and I took the bait - hard. Who wouldn't have? Anyone with "Luv" and

215

"Buttons" in their email address must be a serious, knowledgeable button collector, which made his/her ignorant claim particularly annoying, insulting even. I should have picked-up on the "carnival performer", the "wheel" thing too; it was a reference to "Melvin The Wheel Guy" who does a daily routine at The Wisconsin State Fair, often right in front of the small stand. I send an email reply to Mr. Buttons which will have to go unpublished but is similar in tone and content to the response of Brian (of string-less apron fame) to Mark on that last Sunday a month ago. In retrospect, I'm amazed at Les's work ethic as it applies to messing with his buddies' heads. For me, setting up a regular email account is like going to the dentist, or doing my taxes; this guy does it for fun. But, then again, he also undertakes major apartment remodeling and bicycle overhauling just for yuks, when I wouldn't do either even if I could, which I can't.

I call Les and let him further enjoy his coup, then we talk about big walleyes, the prospects of the Packers and the Eagles, and we say goodbye until next August.

AUTHOR'S COMMENTS

I HAD BEEN WRITING THIS BOOK, WITHOUT BEING AWARE OF doing so, for several years. During days spent at the Wisconsin State Fair my brothers, sister and I have kept alive the memories, now written on these pages, through our resurrection of them in fond discussions. Just as with primitives who tell their oral histories while sitting around a campfire, we continued to keep ours alive, and one could say our campfire was the charcoal grill around which these stories are told, year after year, from generation to generation. Finally, just last year I decided to put it all down on paper for others to, hopefully, enjoy as well.

My six-year old daughter, Juliette, was also instrumental in my getting around to telling our story. For a while now, at bedtime, while lying beside her in her darkened room, she makes her last wish of the night...every night. "Daddy, tell me story when you were little boy - at the State Fair" she says in her child's abbreviated grammar. She's heard them all, the child-sized ones anyway, but never tires of hearing them again - she is, after all, a Mille. And so, I retell stories of a dog riding a motorcycle, of Percheron horses, of her great grandfather who liked to fish but liked to kid around even more. And when she asks me when she will be old enough to work at the State Fair, I tell her this is the year and remind her that her my father would not want her to fill the Cokes too close to the top of the cups.

With regards to the historical accuracy of this effort, I have strived to be as precise as possible while also making no qualms about using exaggeration for effect - that effect being the entertainment of the reader. The greatest license I have taken is to concentrate my contemporary stories - our stories - into a composite timeframe that allows them all to be told within the style I've chosen for this book. On the other hand, the stories from long ago occurred in the actual or approximate timeframes that I've indicated. Dialogue is as it actually occurred, when that is known, or as it was likely to have occurred, knowing the people involved, when it was either before our time or otherwise lost to memory. In all cases, the essence of the many incidents are accurate and the details, in some cases, painstakingly researched; my sister, for example, finally agreed with the accuracy of the Metropolitan Opera experience only after her review of five successive drafts. Early on I considered the technique of composite characters to more efficiently tell our stories, but quickly decided against it, for after all, this book is all about specific people and, while I don't mind concentrating a couple of years of their shenanigans into a single year, to consolidate the people themselves just doesn't seem truthful to me - so I avoided doing so. Grandpa is only grandpa and Roy is…inimitable.

In undertaking a project such as this, a person should expect certain surprises. It was no different for me and, surprises being what they are, I didn't anticipate the direction from which they came. Certainly, one of the bigger revelations was that shared memory is only shared to a degree; beyond a certain point, we each - Toni, Mike, Mark, and I - have different versions of what it was like spending our summer days at the State Fair, our own personal realities, if you will. The reason for this is simple: we were all different ages and, consequently, experienced the Fair from our own separate perspectives. When the rest of us were making the bread runs to Gardetto's with dad Mark was only about three, so that wasn't part of his legacy...and so on. But, at the same time, most of the memories that I've written about are shared by all of us, to one degree or another, and that's what makes them special.

Another unexpected development that came from the writing of this book was the stirring up of long-forgotten feelings and detailed memories. As I sat back in front of my laptop on my long train rides to (and from) Manhattan and allowed the muse to visit, she would occasionally bring along a little gift package, in the form of a long-forgotten impression or detail...the silver barrette in Francie's hair, the mother-of-pearl snaps on the stand-towing cowboy's shirt. But even more unexpected was the surfacing of long forgotten feelings or even, in a few instances, the experiencing of strong emotions that never quite made it to the surface the first time around. I've never been one to wear my heart on my sleeve and I seldom get weepy but, in the writing of the passing of my grandparents and father, I did get all misty... noticeably so, while sitting in a writers' coffee shop just off Philadelphia's Rittenhouse Square one Sunday morning - something which never occurred in the immediacy of 1976, 1982 or 2000. The word cathartic comes to mind.

There are a number of individuals, and sources, who should be recognized for their assistance in the creation of this book. My friends and mini-focus group of sorts, Paul Chung, Kristen Schwecke, Annie Webb, Julie Brown, and Jennifer Arnott each offered valuable feedback and suggestions on various aspects of my efforts. Of primary importance was the booklet 150 YEARS OF THE WISCONSIN STATE FAIR by Jerry Zimmerman, which proved to be an invaluable resource for Wisconsin State Fair related fact-checking, particularly with regards to the dates of certain evolutionary events. Jerry, a Wisconsin State Fair Historian, assisted me both directly and indirectly in this effort. Without his help, this project would have taken much longer and incurred many more long distance calls. I also want to acknowledge photo credits to Rich Rygh of THE CAPITAL TIMES and to the good folks of The Wisconsin State Fair for their support of my project. I have great appreciation, also, for the creative minds - and patience - of Scott Barrie and Sarah Van Male of Cyanotype Book Architects who provided me with a fresh perspective and led me through the unexplored territory of graphic design.

I don't feel it's necessary to further thank the characters described in this book - for several reasons. With regards to my siblings, Toni, Mike, and Mark, while they certainly were helpful, this book is almost as much theirs as it is mine and I only hope they will feel that I have captured the essence of our shared experience. As for wives, children, grandchildren and other kin, the same is true, with a couple of notable exceptions. My oldest daughter Therese (my daughter, the reader) took a break from her book-a-day (or so it seems) rate of literature consumption (I like to think she gets it from me) to act as my initial and ongoing sounding board - I knew if she liked my effort others would as well. If you ever want to know what tomorrow's best sellers will be, just find out what she's reading today. Margaret, my wife, provided me with not only opinion but also patience and support when I needed it most and never complained when I had to find some quiet time to do my writing. And then there are the "near-family" members - Brian, Roy, Les, and all the others, whose day-to-day experiences are key to these pages. My gratitude to them is shown through my attempt to capture their essence as the characters they truly are and, although it may seem that I have a strange way of showing my gratitude, I'm pretty sure they "get it" and appreciate the fond recognition as much as I and my siblings appreciate having them with us at the Fair.

Although my mother plays a small role in this memoir, she was always present in the background. An untold part of her story was an unfulfilled future as a writer. The Catholic nuns at her high school had urged her to accept a journalism scholarship to Alverno College, but, due to the great depression and a need for her to help her family financially, she was unable to pursue that potential. In a small way, therefore, I hope her soul can feel some vicarious fulfillment from this book and, though she's not around to read it, I know she's been looking over my shoulder, nudging me on certain passages that I had struggled with.

Grandma, grandpa, and dad - they're the ones most responsible for creating the family experience this book attempts to describe and I hope my gratitude is reflected in my treatment of them in these pages. I hope, too, that I and the rest of my family will repay our debt to them by continuing to come together at The Wisconsin State Fair for many Augusts to come.

AMATORE MILLE

ABOUT THE AUTHOR

AMATORE "MATT" MILLE WAS BORN AND RAISED IN MILWAUKEE, Wisconsin and currently resides just outside of Philadelphia in Wayne, Pennsylvania. He works as a part-time writer and full-time sales executive in the financial services information technology industry and shares time between his offices in midtown New York and at home. He is married and has two young children, a stepson and three grown children (and five grandchildren) from a previous marriage.

ELEVEN DAYS IN AUGUST is Amatore's first book.

The author can be contacted through Trafford Publishing or, directly, at: **Amatore@comcast.net**

Printed in the United States
by Baker & Taylor Publisher Services